POCKET
ATLAS

KINGFISHER
Kingfisher Publications Plc
New Penderel House
283–288 High Holborn
London WC1V 7HZ

First published by Kingfisher Publications Plc 1997
This edition published in 2000
10 9 8 7 6 5 4 3 2 1
1TR/0200/WKT/HBM(FR)/115MA

A catalogue record for this book is available from
the British Library.

ISBN 0 7534 0142 8

Produced by Miles Kelly Publishing Ltd
Designer: Smiljka Surla
Editors: Rosie Alexander, Samantha Armstrong,
  Angela Royston
Assistant Editor: Susanne Bull
Picture Research: Kate Miles, Yannick Yago

Printed in Hong Kong

POCKET ATLAS

Linda Sonntag

KING*f*ISHER

CONTENTS

INTRODUCTION

W e live in a changing world. Major wars can cause some countries to change their boundaries or even disappear altogether, and new countries to be created. Political events also change the world map. In the 1950s and 1960s, many colonies in Africa and Asia became independent and adopted new names. Another period of massive change occurred during the late 1980s and early 1990s, when the formerly communist Soviet Union changed its policies and decided to break up into 15 separate countries. Around the same time, in eastern Europe, the former communist Federal People's Republic of Yugoslavia split into five countries, while Czechoslovakia was divided into two.

The Pocket Atlas is an essential tool for anyone who wants to study and understand this changing world. It contains maps that show new countries, including those in eastern Europe and the former Soviet Union. There is also information on the geography and history of countries, together with descriptions of how the peoples of the world live and work.

The Atlas begins with a reference section on planet Earth that covers its evolution and life today. The main body of the book contains chapters on the six populated continents and the countries they contain. There is also a special section on Russia and its neighbours, which explains how the former Soviet Union split apart into 15 republics. One of them is Russia, the world's largest country, which lies partly in Europe and partly in Asia. Of the 14 other republics, six are in Europe and eight are in Asia. At the back of the Atlas is a chapter on the icy polar regions and a glossary of technical terms.

The peoples of the world

There are thousands of cultures in the world today, each with its own language. This is what makes the world such a diverse and exciting place in which to live.

Planet Earth

Most scientists believe that the Sun, Earth and other planets formed about 4,600 million years ago (mya) from a huge cloud of tiny solid particles and gases called a nebula. The solid particles and some of the gas had been thrown out of earlier stars that had died. The nebula began to shrink and spin, collapsing inwards because of its own gravity. Soon, material near the centre was colliding at tremendous speeds and giving out so much heat that a glowing star, the Sun, was born. The rest of the nebula formed into a ring around the Sun and collisions inside this ring built up the planets, including our own planet Earth.

For a time the planets were very hot, but they never became hot enough to shine like stars. All the planets were bombarded by other much smaller bodies, so that their surfaces became covered with craters like the ones still seen on the Moon today. On the Earth, however, wind and rain have gradually worn most of the craters away.

Buried deep in the heart of our planet is a metal core of iron and nickel that is larger than the Moon and almost as hot as the surface of the Sun. The outer layer of the core is liquid metal, but enormous pressure at the centre has compressed it into a solid. When Earth formed 4,600 mya, it glowed red hot and the molten metals sank to its centre while the lighter rocks floated to the surface.

Around the core is wrapped a thick layer of hot rock called the mantle. This acts like a heated blanket, holding in the warmth. Around the mantle is a third layer called the crust, which forms the rocky surface of the Earth on which we live. The thickest parts of the crust are about 60 kilometres deep, but if the Earth were compared to an apple, the crust would be only as thick as the apple's skin.

The mantle contains traces of radioactive uranium which steadily gives out heat. This warmth rises, creating a more fluid part of the mantle known as the asthenosphere. Above the

---

■ EARTH FACTS

Diameter at the Equator:
12,756 km
Diameter at the Poles: 12,713 km
Diameter of core: nearly 7,000 km
Thickness of mantle: 2,900 km
Temperature of inner core:
up to 7,000°C
Mass of Earth:
5,900 billion billion tonnes
Average density: 5.5 tonnes/cu m
Land area: 149 million sq km
Ocean area: 361 million sq km
Volume of ocean:
1,321 million cu km
Age: 4,600 million years
Atmosphere: 78% nitrogen,
21% oxygen, 1% argon
Time to rotate on axis:
23 hours 56 minutes
Time to orbit the Sun:
About 365 days 6 hours

partly fluid asthenosphere lies the lithosphere, which includes the outermost mantle and the crust. The lithosphere is made up of massive plates that float on the asthenosphere. These plates are constantly moving, causing the continents to drift apart, mountains to form, the ground to shake and volcanoes to erupt.

The continents reached their present positions around 50 mya and are still slowly drifting as the planet evolves. The Himalayas began to form 40 mya, and continue to be built up and worn gradually away.

Life probably began about 3,500 mya in muddy puddles or along the shores of shallow lakes. Lightning and radiation may have built up simple organic molecules that combined with clay particles to form the first cells. The first living things were microscopic bacteria and algae that grew in large mats by the tide line.

Earth's original atmosphere probably contained large amounts of carbon dioxide, a gas made up of carbon and oxygen. As these early plants developed they used the carbon dioxide to make food and released the oxygen on which all animal life depends. The first animals were jellyfish-like creatures. The first mammals appeared 216 mya, but the first humans did not walk the Earth for another 214 million years.

The Sun will shine for millions more years, but then it will burn up all its fuel and die. The Earth will be left as a cold, lifeless rock.

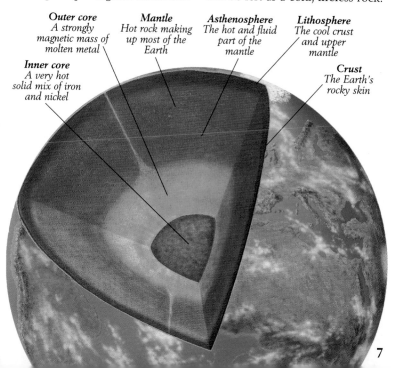

Outer core
A strongly magnetic mass of molten metal

Mantle
Hot rock making up most of the Earth

Asthenosphere
The hot and fluid part of the mantle

Lithosphere
The cool crust and upper mantle

Inner core
A very hot solid mix of iron and nickel

Crust
The Earth's rocky skin

The Solar System

The Earth belongs to a family of nine planets, each of which is in orbit (circling) around the Sun. Together they make up the Solar System, which also includes the moons orbiting around their planets, lumps of rock called asteroids and comets with their long tails of dust and gas.

The Sun, the star at the centre of the Solar System, is a burning hot ball of shining gas. Without its heat and light the Earth would be a frozen dead world. Among the nine planets that orbit the Sun, the Earth is unique. Only the Earth has water in its oceans and enough oxygen to support animal life. Mercury, Venus, Mars and Pluto are rocky wastes. The giant planets Jupiter, Saturn, Uranus and Neptune are globes of gas and ice particles. The Earth is habitable because it is at just the right distance from the Sun. A little closer and it would resemble scorching Venus.

A little further away and it would be a permanently frozen waste.

However, the Earth has not always been as it is now. Soon after it formed, about 4,600 million years ago (mya), this planet was a roasting cauldron. Over millions of years the surface cooled and the atmosphere, oceans and continents formed.

Life began in the still tropically warm oceans about 3,500 mya with microscopic life-forms. Many scientists believe that the first animals and plants began to develop and live on land about 400 mya.

Mercury

Earth

Venus

Mars

Sun

Jupiter

Outside our Solar System are other solar systems that have developed around other stars as hot as our Sun. Many scientists believe that intelligent life must exist on other planets like our Earth. Some scientists hope to find other inhabited planets by picking up radio signals sent out by any alien civilizations that may exist. A project called the Search for Extra-Terrestrial Intelligence (SETI), has been trying to identify signals from space that sound artificial. So far it has been unsuccessful.

Other scientists have sent out radio messages from Earth in the hope of a reply. Some space probes have plaques on their sides showing the position of Earth. Others have electronically encoded pictures, greetings and music. It is hoped that as they drift out of our Solar System and into others, alien spacecraft may intercept them because they want to find out about life on other planets such as ours.

Pluto

Neptune

Uranus

Saturn

■ EARTH FACTS
Circumference around the Equator:
40,075 km
Circumference around the Poles:
40,007 km
Distance to the centre of the Earth:
About 6,370 km
Surface area:
About 510,065,600 sq km
Average distance from the Sun:
149,600,000 km
Rotation speed: 1,660 km per hour
at the Equator
Speed in orbit: 29.8 km per second
Average distance from the Moon:
385,000 km
Chief elements of the Earth's crust:
Oxygen (46.6%), silicon (27.7%),
aluminium (8.1%), iron (5%)

World facts and figure

T he surface of the Earth is about 70 per cent water and 30 per cent land. The largest ocean is the Pacific, which is larger than all the land put together. Asia is the largest continent. It covers nearly a third of the total land area.

■ EARTH EXTREMES

Hottest shade temperature recorded: 57.7° at Al'Aziziyah, Libya, on 13.9.22

Coldest temperature recorded: -89.92 at Vostock, Antarctica, on 21.7.83

Highest annual rainfall: 11,770 mm at Tutunendo, Colombia

Most rain in one month: 9,300 mm at Cherrapunji, India, in July 1861

Driest place on Earth: Near Calama, Atacama Desert, Chile (0 mm)

Most snow in one year: 31,102 mm on Mt Rainier, Washington State, USA, 1971–1972

Greatest tides: 16.3 m in Bay of Fundy, Nova Scotia, Canada

Strongest surface wind recorded: 372 km/h at Mt Washington, New Hampshire, USA, 1934

Greatest ocean depth: 11,033 m, Marianas Trench, Pacific Ocean

Deepest gorge: 2,400 m, Hells Canyon, Idaho, USA

Longest gorge: 349 km, Grand Canyon, Arizona, USA

Highest navigated lake: Titicaca, Peru/Bolivia, 3,811 m above sea level

Deepest lake: Baikal, Siberia, Russia, 1,940 m

■ OCEANS

Pacific, 181,000,000 sq km
Atlantic, 106,000,000 sq km
Indian, 73,490,000 sq km
Arctic, 14,350,000 sq km

■ LONGEST RIVERS

Nile, Africa, 6,670 km
Amazon, S. America, 6,448 km
Mississippi-Missouri-Red Rock, N. America, 6,231 km
Yenisey, Russia, 5,540 km
Chang Jiang, China, 5,470 km
Ob-Irtysh, Russia, 5,150 km
Lena, Russia, 4,828 km
Congo, Africa, 4,828 km
Amur, Asia, 4,506 km
Huang He, China, 4,345 km
Mekong, S.E. Asia, 4,184 km
Niger, Africa, 4,184 km

Traditional feluccas sail on the river Nile.

■ DESERTS

Sahara, 8,400,000 sq km
Australian Desert, 1,550,000 sq km
Arabian Desert, 1,300,000 sq km
Gobi, 1,040,000 sq km
Kalahari, 520,000 sq km

Sand dunes are shaped by desert winds.

■ MAJOR WATERFALLS
Highest:
Angel Falls, Venezuela, 979 m
Tugela Falls, South Africa, 948 m
Yosemite Falls, California, USA,
  739 m
Greatest volume:
Boyoma Falls, Zaire, 17,000 cu m/sec
Niagara, N. America, 6,000 cu m/sec

*Adventurers bungee-jump off
Angel Falls.*

■ LARGEST ISLANDS
Greenland, N. Atlantic,
  2,175,600 sq km
New Guinea, S.W. Pacific,
  794,090 sq km
Borneo, S.W. Pacific, 751,078 sq km
Madagascar, Indian Ocean,
  587,040 sq km
Baffin Island, Canadian Arctic,
  476,066 sq km
Sumatra, Indian Ocean,
  431,982 sq km
Honshu, N.W. Pacific,
  230,822 sq km
Great Britain, N. Atlantic,
  229,522 sq km
Ellesmere Island, Canadian Arctic,
  198,393 sq km
Victoria Island, Canadian Arctic,
  192,695 sq km

■ HIGHEST MOUNTAINS
Asia:
Everest, Himalaya – Nepal, 8,848 m
K2 (Godwin Austen), Karakoram,
  China/Pakistan/India, 8,611 m
Kanchenjunga, Himalaya – Nepal,
  8,470 m
Makalu, Himalaya – Nepal, 8,470 m
Dhaulagiri, Himalaya – Nepal,
  8,172 m
Nanga Parbat, Himalaya – India,
  8,126 m
Annapurna, Himalaya – Nepal,
  8,075 m
South America:
Aconcagua, Andes – Argentina,
  6,960 m
North America:
McKinley, Alaska – USA, 6,194 m
Africa:
Kilimanjaro – Tanzania, 5,895 m
Europe:
Elbrus, Caucasus – Russia, 5,633 m
Mont Blanc, Alps – France, 4,810 m
Antarctica:
Vinson Massif, 5,139 m
Australasia:
Wilhelm, Bismarck – New Guinea,
  4,694 m

*Snow covers the summit of
Mount Everest.*

How maps are made

The oldest surviving maps were made by the Babylonians, who lived in modern-day Iraq more than 4,000 years ago. Many ancient map-makers thought that the Earth was flat, but the first sea voyages around the world in the 1600s led to a great improvement in the accuracy of map-making.

The only really accurate map of the world is a globe, which is round like the Earth itself. Map-makers use a technique called projection to show the curved surface of the Earth on flat maps of continents and countries. It is impossible for all areas, shapes, distances and directions to be drawn accurately on a flat map, so map projections are worked out mathematically to preserve chosen features. For example, Mercator's projection distorts areas in order to maintain directions, so that it can be used for navigation.

Map-makers drew imaginary lines around the Earth in a grid to help the map-reader find places. These are lines of latitude and longitude. Lines of latitude run horizontally across the globe. The line where the Earth's circumference is at its greatest is called the Equator. Parallel lines of latitude are drawn north and south of the Equator.

Lines of longitude divide the Earth up through its Poles, like the segments of an orange. Each line is a great circle going right round the Earth. Lines of longitude have no obvious reference point, such as the Equator, so English navigators made their home port, Greenwich, on the River Thames near London, the line of zero degrees longitude. Longitude is still measured east and west of this prime meridian.

Early navigators used the stars to find out their position. Latitude was calculated from the heights of the stars in the sky or the position of the Sun as it rose,

Zone photographed from one flight path

Flight path of aircraft

Area covered by previous photograph

Area covered by one photograph

Maps from aerial photographs

Aerial photographs were first used for map making during World War I. Modern aerial photographs are taken with a 60% overlap. When pairs of photographs are viewed stereoscopically, the land appears in 3D and contours can be plotted.

set or reached its zenith (highest point). Longitude can also be measured against the stars, but it is necessary to know the exact time, because the stars move east to west across the sky. In the mid-1700s an English navigator, John Harrison, invented an instrument called the marine chronometer.

This made it possible to measure longitude accurately, so that more accurate maps could be made. By comparing local time, measured from the angle of the Sun, with Greenwich mean time on the chronometer, the navigator could work out how far east or west he was from the prime meridian.

Mercator's projection (cylindrical)

Conical projection

Zenithal or azimuthal projection

Peters' projection (equal area)

Goode's projection (interrupted equal area)

Map projections
● ● ● ● ● ● ● ● ● ●

The principle of Mercator's projection is shown by wrapping a piece of paper around the Equator to form a cylinder. The landmasses have the right shape, but are stretched towards the Poles. In Peters' projection landmasses have correct areas, but their shape is squashed.

In a zenithal projection the paper remains flat and touches the globe at one Pole, so that lines of longitude show their correct angles. A conical projection, in which the paper is rolled into a cone and placed over the globe to touch it along one line of latitude, shows countries with the minimum distortion. In Goode's projection the oceans have been opened up to show the continents. No projection is fully accurate. The globe is the only truly accurate world map.

13

Environment

The environment is the surroundings in which we live. Some parts of it are living, such as plants, animals and people, while other parts are non-living, such as air and water. All these elements work together to keep life going.

People have always had an effect on the environment, but today human activities are causing serious damage. The air is being polluted with harmful gases from vehicles and factories. Water is polluted with pesticides, industrial waste and domestic sewage. Forests are cut down for timber and to make way for farmland, which is causing many plants and animals to die out.

Air pollution can damage the Earth's atmosphere and affect the climate. Chemicals called chlorofluorocarbons (CFCs) are destroying the ozone layer, a protective barrier around the Earth that keeps out harmful

Deforestation

When trees are cleared from high ground rainwater rushes downhill, taking soil with it. It floods the ground below and causes rivers to silt up. In the dry season the soil bakes hard and cracks.

radiation from the Sun. Pollution from burning coal, oil and car exhausts increases the greenhouse effect, a process that traps heat from the Sun to warm the Earth. Many scientists believe that this pollution is already making the Earth warmer. If the overall temperature of the world rose by just three degrees, the ice caps at the North and South Poles would melt, causing sea levels to rise and flood many areas.

Habitat destruction is the greatest threat to plant and animal species worldwide. Sometimes forests are cleared to make way for agriculture or housing. However, forests are

Oil spills

Many people volunteer to help animals in danger. If there is an oil spill, the lives of thousands of animals and birds may be at risk. Teams work hard to clean them so that they can be returned to the wild.

vitally important to the environment as a whole. They act as a water-holding system. Without them rivers run faster in rainy seasons, causing soil erosion in their upper reaches and problems of silting as the river approaches the sea. In many areas erosion is robbing the land of nutrients so that deserts continue to spread.

Coral reefs, mangrove swamps and the entire wetland ecosystem – rivers, streams, lakes, ponds and marshes – are also under threat. Many types of wildlife are being lost as dams are built to produce power, marshes drained for agricultural land and tropical swamps cleared for shrimp farms. Surviving wetlands are often damaged by engineering schemes, by pollution from industrial waste, or by thermal pollution from water used for cooling. Another problem is eutrophication. This occurs when nutrients from chemical fertilizers flow off the land and cause ponds and rivers to be choked by a huge growth of weeds.

Governments are being urged to find ways of reducing pollution and conserving the environment to prevent irreparable damage. However, economic and political considerations are often put first. The safety of the planet and of human life is often ignored. The worst ever nuclear accident, in 1986 at Chernobyl, Ukraine, frightened the world. But even the regular disposal of nuclear waste from power stations remains a major problem. Nuclear waste can remain lethal (deadly) for thousands of years and no one yet knows how or where to dispose of it safely and permanently.

Traffic pollution

This baby in its pushchair is directly exposed to traffic exhaust. Exhaust fumes cause severe breathing problems and can be lethal. Governments are looking at new ways of reducing traffic pollution.

Recycling

Every household can save energy, time and raw resources by recycling some of its rubbish, including newspapers, glass and cans. These materials can be broken down and used again.

Population

There are well over 5,600 million people living in the world today and the number is expected to grow to over 9,000 million by 2050. Some parts have far more people than others. These are mostly regions where there is fertile agricultural land, such as China, or where big industrial cities have grown up, as has happened in many European countries. From time to time populations change in size. War, drought, famine and disease may kill huge numbers of people or drive them from their homes. Poverty can force whole communities to move elsewhere in search of a better life.

Populations also grow at different rates. Most Europeans and North Americans are now living longer than ever before because they have good supplies of food and healthcare. However, most of these people are choosing to have fewer children, so the population is growing very slowly. By contrast, in Africa, South America and Asia, the population is growing rapidly. Many people there lack good food, clean water, medical care and sanitation. These problems may become even worse if population growth is not controlled. In China strict legislation limits the number of children a woman may have.

The World Health Organization (WHO), which is

These tables compare countries by area and population. If population growth is not controlled, some countries may face serious problems in feeding and caring for their people.

■ LARGEST COUNTRIES
  BY AREA
Russia: 17,075,400 sq km
Canada: 9,970,610 sq km
China: 9,572,900 sq km
United States: 9,372,571 sq km
Brazil: 8,511,999 sq km
Australia: 7,713,364 sq km
India: 3,287,500 sq km
Argentina: 2,870,092 sq km
Kazakhstan: 2,717,300 sq km
Sudan: 2,505,810 sq km

■ LARGEST COUNTRIES
  BY POPULATION
China: 1,205,181,000
India: 913,600,000
United States: 260,529,000
Indonesia: 189,907,000
Brazil: 159,143,000
Russia: 148,366,000
Pakistan: 126,284,000
Japan: 124,959,000
Bangladesh: 122,210,000
Nigeria: 119,328,000

North America

South America

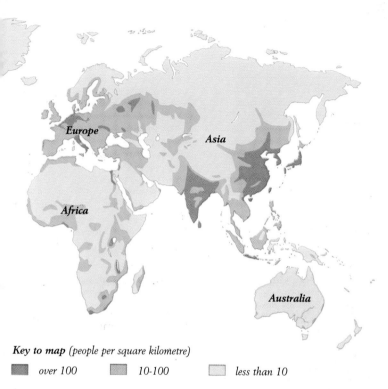

Key to map *(people per square kilometre)*

over 100   10-100   *less than 10*

part of the United Nations, aims to improve standards of health and health education around the world. The WHO works with governments to provide safe drinking water and adequate sewage disposal. Vaccination programmes are now carried out in most countries. Eighty per cent of the world's children are now immunized against the killer diseases of polio, tuberculosis, measles, diphtheria, tetanus and whooping cough.

Most of the world's governments carry out population surveys called censuses, which not only count the number of people, but also record where they live and what sort of job they do. These statistics help countries to measure changes in population and plan for the future.

Key to chart

Asia 3,380 million
Africa 697 million
Europe (including Russia) 733 million
North and Central America 449 million
South America 316 million
Oceania 28 million

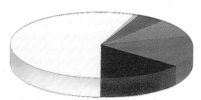

17

Government

A**ll countries have governments that decide how the country is run.** They make laws, set taxes and spend public money on projects and services of national importance, such as education and defence. Governments have the power to go to war against other countries, though sometimes their decisions may be challenged or changed by public opinion. Governments also have the power to make agreements with other governments. A typical example of this is a trade agreement where countries benefit from selling goods to one another. They can also impose sanctions (economic restrictions) on other governments by either banning trade or taxing imports.

Today most countries are democratic republics. This means the people have elected their government from a choice of political parties and have also elected their head of state. The opposite of a democracy is a dictatorship, a form of government in which one person or a small group of people has absolute power. In a dictatorship there are no elections and people are not free to choose a political party to support. Dictatorships are often run by the army or a monarch.

Communist countries are usually run by one political party, the Communist Party, which believes that everyone should have equal shares in the country's property and wealth, and all jobs should be equal. In communist

United Nations

The General Assembly of the United Nations (UN) meets in New York. The UN works towards world peace.

The Berlin Wall

Germans celebrate becoming one nation again by demolishing the Berlin Wall on 3 October 1990. Germany was divided from 1945 to 1990 into East and West.

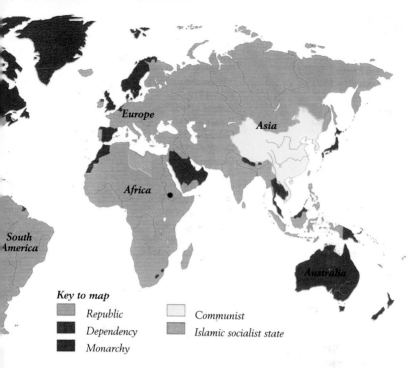

Key to map

- Republic
- Dependency
- Monarchy
- Communist
- Islamic socialist state

countries the economy is directed by the state, which owns and runs businesses, industries and farms. Private enterprise, in which individuals and groups own and run their own businesses, is not allowed.

A free market is the opposite of a communist economy. This is an economic system which is not directed by the state, and which encourages private enterprise. States that have both public and private ownership are said to have a mixed economy.

Most of the world's governments send representatives to the United Nations (UN) in New York. The UN helps the countries of the world to keep in touch with one another.

> ■ **TERMS**
> *These are some of the terms used to describe the way a country is governed.*
> **Monarchy:** A country where the head of the state is a monarch (a king or a queen). In a modern constitutional monarchy the monarch's power to govern is strictly limited.
> **Republic:** The opposite of a monarchy, in which the country's head of state is often an elected president.
> **Democracy:** Any form of government that is elected by popular vote. In a multi-party democracy voters choose between two or more political parties.
> **Federal state:** The power in federal states is divided between one central and several regional governments.
> **Dependency:** A state ruled by another country.

Religion

S ince prehistoric times, people everywhere have tried to make sense of the world around them. This search for a meaning to life grew into religious belief. The first religions were based on the worship of natural forces, such as air, fire and wind, or animals, mountains and rivers. These became linked to powerful supernatural beings – gods and goddesses, spirits and demons.

The Greeks worshipped a mother goddess, patron of fertility and the harvest whom they called Hera. Her consort was Zeus, most powerful of all the gods, and their home was Mount Olympus, the highest peak in Greece. Beyond Olympus was the underworld (the realm of the dead), which was ruled by Hades and his consort Persephone. Roman religion gave the Greek gods

Jerusalem, Israel

Orthodox Jews stand at prayer by Jerusalem's western wall, a holy place called the Wailing Wall.

different names. In addition, every household had its guardian spirits, called the lares and penates, and each person had their own protective spirit or genius.

Today some religions, such as Hinduism, have many gods. Others, such as Islam, Judaism and Christianity, have only one god. The Chinese religion of Confucianism has no gods at all.

Many religions have developed from older faiths. Christianity sprang from Judaism. Religions are often divided into different groups whose members believe in the same principles, but may interpret them in different ways. Christianity, for example, includes Protestant, Roman Catholic and Eastern Orthodox groups.

Religion has played a major role in shaping world history and remains a powerful force. Today there are hundreds of religions. Although they may differ widely, they all teach their followers to live by a moral code, which means knowing the difference between right and wrong.

Worship

This chart shows how people worshipped at the beginning of the 1990s. The largest group is Christian, followed by Muslim and Hindu.

- Christian 33.5%
- No religion 20.7%
- Muslim 18.2%
- Hindu 13.5%
- Other 7.3%
- Buddhist 6%
- Sikh 0.4%
- Jewish 0.3%
- Shinto 0.1%

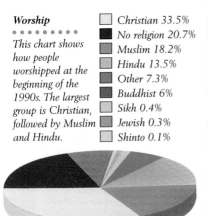

Christianity

Christianity is based on the teachings of Jesus Christ, who was born in Palestine. Christians believe that Jesus is the son of God and that he rose from the dead after being crucified on a cross. The Bible includes Jewish and Christian teachings.

Islam

Islam was founded in Arabia by the prophet Muhammad in about AD622. The Muslims' (followers of Islam) most sacred book is the Koran, which is the direct word of the one God, Allah. Islamic life is based on a set of rules called the five pillars of Islam.

Hinduism

Hinduism is the major religion of India. It began in about 1500BC. Hindus worship many gods. The three most important are Shiva, Vishnu and Brahma. They believe in rebirth of the soul after death (reincarnation) and are born into social castes.

Buddhism

Buddhism is based on the teachings of an Indian prince, Gautama Siddharta, born in 563BC. He became known as Buddha, or Enlightened One. Buddhists believe in reincarnation and nirvana (peace). They meditate to achieve understanding.

Confucianism

Confucianism has no gods or belief in life after death, but stresses good conduct. It follows the teachings of Confucius, who was born in China about 551BC. Taoism, another Chinese religion, began about 300BC. Its many gods are taken from folk religions.

Judaism

Judaism was the first religion to teach that there is one God. Its main laws come from the Torah, the first five books of the Hebrew Bible. The ancient religion of the Jews was founded by Abraham, a Hebrew who lived in Canaan around 2000BC.

Sikhism

Sikhism was founded in India in the late 1400s by Guru (teacher) Nanak. The Sikhs believe in only one God. Sikh men wear five 'k' symbols. They are kesh (uncut hair), kangha (comb), kara (bracelet), kaccha (breeches), and finally kirpan (dagger).

Shintoism

Shintoists worship the spirits of animals, rocks, trees, springs and other elements of nature. Shinto is Japan's oldest religion. Until the mid-1900s the Japanese also worshipped their emperor, believing he was descended from the powerful Sun goddess.

NORTH AMERICA

North America is shaped like a giant triangle. The far north extends well above the Arctic Circle and is a frozen, treeless land. The continent's highest point, Denali (Mount McKinley), lies to the north in Alaska. The extreme south has both dry deserts and lush rainforests, with tropical vegetation covering many of the Caribbean islands. In between lie the forests of Canada and the northern United States of America. To the east the five Great Lakes form part of the continent's water drainage system. Vast prairielands of wheat spread right across the centre of North America.

Constant movement of the Earth's crust causes earthquakes from time to time. California's Death Valley, the lowest point in North America, lies in an earthquake zone. This movement of the crust has also shaped the Rocky Mountains and the other great ranges that run down the western side of the continent, and is still shaping them today.

North America includes countries with all kinds of cultures, languages and economies. These very different countries all have one thing in common – they were all controlled by a European power at one time. The countries of the North American mainland are now independent, but European links continue on some islands. The continent's largest island, Greenland, is a self-governing province of Denmark.

Bald eagle

The bald eagle is the national symbol of the USA. It is found only in North America, and is a protected species.

■ CONTINENTAL FACTS
Area: 24,249,000 sq km (including North and Central America, the Caribbean and Greenland)
Population: 449,000,000 people
Independent countries: 23
Largest country: Canada
Smallest country: St Kitts and Nevis
Highest point: Denali (Mount McKinley), Alaska, USA, 6,194 m
Lowest point: Death Valley, California, USA, 86 m below sea level
Largest lake: Lake Superior, Canada/USA, 83,270 sq km
Longest rivers: Mississippi-Missouri-Red Rock, USA, 5970 km. Mackenzie-Peace, Canada, 4,216 km

Totem pole

Characters from Native American folklore are represented on traditional carved wooden totem poles in Canada.

Food and culture

Tortillas have been a basic Mexican food since before the time of the Aztec civilization. They are thin pancakes of maize or wheat flour. Tortillas can be eaten plain or stuffed with salad.

Canada

■ CANADA
Area: 9,970,610 sq km
Population: 28,436,000
Capital: Ottawa (921,000)
Official languages: English, French
Currency: Canadian dollar
Main exports: Vehicles, petroleum,
aluminium, timber, wood pulp,
wheat

ARCTIC OCEAN

Ellesmere Island

Banks Island

Victoria Island

ALASKA (U.S.A.)

Porcupine

Dawson

YUKON TERRITORY

Mackenzie

Great Bear Lake

NORTHERN TERRITORIES

Mt. Logan 5959m

★ Whitehorse

Liard

Yellowknife

Great Slave Lake

Canadian Shield

CANADA

BRITISH COLUMBIA

Peace

Prince Rupert

Peace River

ALBERTA

SASKATCHEWAN

Churc

MANITO

NORTH PACIFIC OCEAN

Mt. Robson 3954m

Fraser

Edmonton ★

N. Saskatchewan

Prince Albert

Rocky Mountains

Calgary

Saskatoon

Lak Winni

Vancouver Island

Vancouver

Medicine Hat

S. Saskatchewan

Victoria ★

Regina ★

Winnipeg ★

UNITED STATES OF AMERICA

N

0 100 200 300 400 500 600 700 800 Kilometres
0 100 200 300 400 500 Miles

C anada's northern lands
reach deep into the
frozen Arctic, but most
of the population lives in the
south, close to the border with
the USA. The country consists
of ten provinces and two
territories. It is full of
contrasts, from fishing
villages scattered along the
Atlantic coast to major
centres such as the French-
speaking city of Montreal. The
central plains form an
immense grain-growing area,
while rain-washed forests border
the Pacific Ocean.

Canada was once a farming
nation. Agriculture is still
important, but now the country is
highly industrialized and produces
all kinds of manufactured goods.

Baffin
Bay

Baffin Island

Davis Strait

Labrador
Sea

Hudson
Bay

Feuilles

NEWFOUNDLAND

NORTH
ATLANTIC
OCEAN

● Goose Bay

**Island of
Newfoundland**

Severn

James Bay

QUEBEC

★
St. John's

ONTARIO

Albany

St. Lawrence River

**NEW
BRUNSWICK**

**PRINCE
EDWARD
ISLAND**

Quebec★

★ Fredericton

St John ●

★ Halifax

**NOVA
SCOTIA**

Montreal
●

Lake
Superior

■OTTAWA

Lake
Huron

Lake
Ontario

Toronto★

Lake Erie

25

People and history

The Inuit people (Eskimos) were among the earliest inhabitants of Canada. Their word for community, *kanata*, gave Canada its name. The country itself has become a collection of communities. In the 1400s and 1500s the French and British came. They claimed lands in the east, attracted by rich fishing grounds and the chance to trade in furs. After bitter struggles during the 1700s, Britain took most of the French land and created two colonies, one English-speaking, the other French-speaking. These colonies were united as one nation in 1867.

Towards the future

Today almost half of all Canadians have British ancestors, while the other half are of French descent. The eastern province of Quebec is the centre of French culture – over 75 per cent of its population are French Canadians. In recent decades many French Canadians have campaigned for Quebec to become a separate nation. In 1992 the Inuit people, who live in the north, were granted a self-governing homeland called Nunavut, which will come into being in 1999.

Economy

Canada is a prosperous country. Most of its wealth comes from developing what occurs naturally – trees, fish, oil, natural gas, minerals and water. It is the world's largest exporter of timber, paper and other forest products. As well as being rich in all kinds of fish, Canada's huge lakes and rivers are dammed to provide electricity. Canada has a highly modernized manufacturing industry, producing everything from cars to canned fruit. However, most of the workforce is employed in service industries such as education and finance.

Eastern Canada
● ● ● ● ● ● ● ● ● ● ● ● ● ●

A Nova Scotian boy learns to play the bagpipes. Nova Scotia means 'New Scotland' and many of its people preserve the old Scottish ways.

Baffin Island
● ●

Baffin Island in the Canadian Arctic is the home of Inuit people. They live in modern well insulated buildings but still use traditional kayaks or canoes.

Western Canada

The spectacular Athabasca Glacier is part of Jasper National Park, high up in the snow-capped Rocky Mountains in Alberta. It attracts many visitors from all over Canada and abroad.

Geography

Canada has more lakes and inland waters than any other country in the world. Forests cover almost half the country's total land area. The Coast Mountains and the snow-capped Rocky Mountains dominate western Canada. Beyond the Rockies the landscape softens into the Great Plains, with evergreen forests in the north and prairies in the south. Bordering the plains is a gigantic plateau called the Canadian Shield, which is made up of some of the oldest rocks in the world. To the far north, Canada extends to the frozen wastes of the Arctic Circle.

The space industry

The Canadarm is a robotic arm used on space shuttles. It is lifting an astronaut out of the shuttle to work on a satellite. Canada has a thriving space industry.

CN Tower

At 553 m tall, the CN Tower is the world's tallest self-supporting structure. It stands on the waterfront in Toronto, overlooking Lake Ontario.

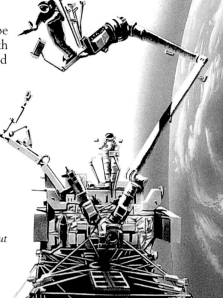

United States
of America

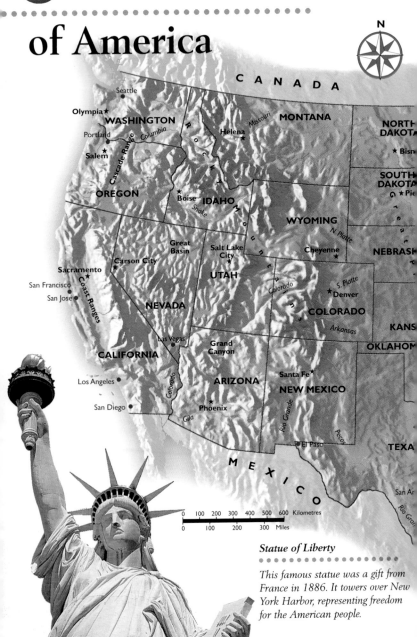

N

CANADA

Seattle
Olympia ★
WASHINGTON
Portland ★
Columbia
Salem ★
Cascade Range
Helena ★
MONTANA
Missouri

NORTH DAKOTA
★ Bisn

OREGON
★ Boise **IDAHO**
Snake

SOUTH DAKOTA
∩ ★ Pie

WYOMING
N. Platte
Cheyenne ★

NEBRASK

Great Basin
Salt Lake City ★
Sacramento ★
Carson City ★
UTAH
Colorado
S. Platte
★ Denver

San Francisco ●
Coast Ranges
San Jose ●
NEVADA
COLORADO
Arkansas

KANS

Las Vegas ●
Grand Canyon
OKLAHOM

CALIFORNIA
Los Angeles ●
Colorado
ARIZONA
Santa Fe ★
NEW MEXICO

San Diego ●
★ Phoenix
Gila
Rio Grande

● El Paso
Pecos
TEXA

MEXICO

San Ar
Rio Gra

0 100 200 300 400 500 600 Kilometres
0   100   200   300 Miles

Statue of Liberty

This famous statue was a gift from France in 1886. It towers over New York Harbor, representing freedom for the American people.

■ **UNITED STATES**
Area: 9,372,571 sq km
Population: 260,529,000
Capital: Washington DC (607,000)
Official language: English
Currency: US dollar
Main exports: Aircraft, vehicles, chemicals, coal, machinery, maize, oil, soya beans, wheat

MAINE
★ Augusta

VERMONT
Montpelier ★
NEW HAMPSHIRE
Concord ★

MASSACHUSETTS
Lake Huron
Lake Ontario
★ Boston

MINNESOTA
Lake Superior

WISCONSIN
nneapolis
St Paul
Lake Michigan
MICHIGAN
Lansing ★
Detroit ★
Lake Erie
Buffalo
NEW YORK
Albany ★
Hartford ★
RHODE IS.
■ Providence
CONNECTICUT

Madison ★
Milwaukee ●
Cleveland ●
PENNSYLVANIA
New York City

Des Moines
★
Chicago ●
Toledo ●
OHIO
Columbus ★
Pittsburgh ●
Harrisburg ★
NEW JERSEY
★ Trenton
Philadelphia ●

IOWA
ILLINOIS
INDIANA
Indianapolis ★
Cincinnati ●
Ohio
WEST VIRGINIA
Baltimore ●
DELAWARE
★ Dover
WASHINGTON D.C.

coln
Kansas City
Jefferson City ★
Springfield ★
St. Louis ●
Frankfort ★
Charleston ★
VIRGINIA
Richmond ★
MARYLAND
Annapolis ★

peka
MISSOURI
KENTUCKY
Winston-Salem ●
NORTH CAROLINA
★ Raleigh

ARKANSAS
Memphis ●
Nashville ★
TENNESSEE
Tennessee
SOUTH CAROLINA
★ Columbia

homa ty
Arkansas
Little Rock ★
MISSISSIPPI
Alabama
Atlanta ★
GEORGIA
NORTH ATLANTIC OCEAN

River
Montgomery ★
ALABAMA
Jacksonville ●

allas
LOUISIANA
Mississippi
Jackson ★
Baton Rouge ★
Tallahassee ★

In
Houston ●
New Orleans ●
FLORIDA

Gulf of Mexico
Miami ●

Appalachian Mountains

The space shuttle
● ● ● ● ● ● ● ● ● ● ● ● ● ● ● ● ● ● ● ●
The USA pioneered the reusable space shuttle. It is launched on the back of a huge fuel tank powered by booster rockets.

T he United States of America (USA) stretches a third of the way around the Earth, crossing eight time zones. The country is divided into 50 states. Two of these are isolated from the rest – Alaska, on Canada's western edge, and Hawaii, an island chain in the North Pacific Ocean.

The USA is ruled according to its famous Constitution, a document setting out how the country is governed. It allows individual states within the union to make some of their own laws. This helps each state to keep its individual character.

No other country in the world contains so much variety within its borders, from the icy lands of Alaska and the scorched deserts of the southwest, to the wide plains in the Midwest, the spectacular rock formations of Arizona and the subtropical forests of the southeast.

KAUAI
●Kapaa
NIIHAU

OAHU
Kaneohe
Honolulu★   MOLOKAI
Kualapuu Lahaina
LANAI   MAUI
KAHOOLAWE

Mauna Kea
4205m ▲ Hilo
HAWAII   ▲ Mauna Loa
4169m

Mountains and plains

The USA has two great mountain chains, the forested Appalachian Mountains in the east and the snow-capped Rocky Mountains in the west. Massive plains stretch across the country between them. The northern and central parts of the plain are known as the Midwest. Much of this area is fertile farmland, with rich soil watered by major rivers such as the Mississippi, Missouri and Ohio. These rivers are part of a water drainage system that includes the five Great Lakes in the northeast.

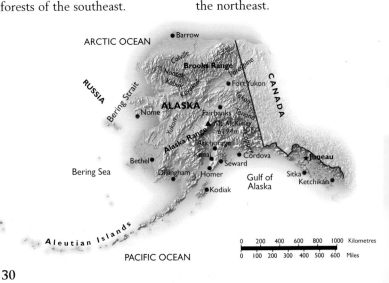

ARCTIC OCEAN ● Barrow
Colville
Brooks Range
Noatak   Porcupine
RUSSIA Kobuk Koyukuk ● Fort Yukon CANADA
Bering Strait
●Nome ALASKA Yukon
Fairbanks ●
Tanana
Mt. McKinley Tanana
6194m
Alaska Range Anchorage
Kenai ● ● Cordova
Bethel●   ● Seward   ★Juneau
Dillingham● Homer Gulf of Sitka
Bering Sea ●Kodiak Alaska Ketchikan●

A l e u t i a n   I s l a n d s

PACIFIC OCEAN

| 0 | 200 | 400 | 600 | 800 | 1000 Kilometres |
| 0 | 100 | 200 | 300 | 400 | 500 | 600 Miles |

Citrus fruits

The USA is the world's leading grower of citrus fruits. Florida produces two thirds of the sweet oranges and grapefruit grown in the USA.

Climate

Almost a third of Alaska lies north of the Arctic Circle, and some of this land is permanently frozen. The Midwest experiences floods and fierce tornadoes. All the southern states have hot summers and mild, or even warm, winters. In the southeast the climate is humid, with storms along the coast. However, there is little rainfall in the southwest, where deserts cover much of the land. In Hawaii, far out in the Pacific Ocean, the tropical climate hardly changes all year.

The White House

The White House in the city of Washington DC is the official residence of the president of the USA.

The frozen north

The people of Alaska traditionally cross the ice and snow in sledges drawn by packs of husky dogs. The modern form of transport is the skidoo, a motorized vehicle that runs on caterpillar tracks and skis.

Wheatfields near Correll

Rolling prairielands of wheat stretch as far as the eye can see all around the small town of Correll, near Des Moines in Minnesota. Wheat is grown on a massive scale in America's fertile Midwest. During the harvest, combines travel in line for many days.

31

Birth of the USA

The first inhabitants of the USA were the American Indians. They lived here for 40,000 years before Europeans arrived in the 1500s.

By the 1700s British settlers had established 13 colonies on the east coast, which were ruled from Britain. When the colonies objected to British rule, the American Revolutionary War (1775-1783) broke out with Britain. The colonies won this war and became known as states. The USA was born. In 1787 the law of the land was drawn up. It was called the Constitution and still applies today.

The land of the free

From 1861 to 1865 a Civil War raged between the southern and northern states. The south wanted individual states to have more power and the right to use African slaves. The north won the war and slavery was finally abolished. Since then people from all over the world have settled in the USA. Steady population growth has helped to make it a very powerful country.

Chicago
. . . .

Two bascule bridges, operated by weights, rise to let ships pass on the Chicago River. In the centre of the picture behind the first bridge is the Wrigley Building, Chicago's most famous landmark.

Jambalaya
. . . .

Jambalaya is a spicy rice and prawn dish from New Orleans in the Deep South. It blends French and African cookery.

Monument Valley
. . . .

Millions of years of wind and rain have carved the dramatic rock shapes of Monument Valley in the southwest of the USA.

Leading the world

The USA has enormous economic power and leads the world in the production of manufactured goods. Its products include aircraft, electronic goods, cars and chemicals. However, industries that produce services rather than goods are now the largest part of the economy of the USA. These include property, finance, insurance, entertainment and healthcare.

The country's economy is largely based on a free market system. Companies are encouraged to compete against each other to win trade. Shares in companies are bought and sold at the New York Stock Exchange on Wall Street.

The enormous size of the USA has always been a great advantage. The land yields large amounts of natural resources such as petroleum, natural gas, coal and metal ores as well as fresh water. Vast forests meet most of the country's timber needs and many of its large rivers have been dammed to produce hydro-electric power.

Agriculture

Agriculture earns much less income than manufacturing and service industries, but is still carried out on a grand scale. The large farms of the Midwestern plains have made the USA the world's leading food producer. It is almost self-sufficient, unlike other countries that have to import food to feed their population. Kansas has earned the name 'breadbasket of America' because it produces so much wheat. Other products include beef, dairy foods, soya beans, cotton and tobacco.

Central America and

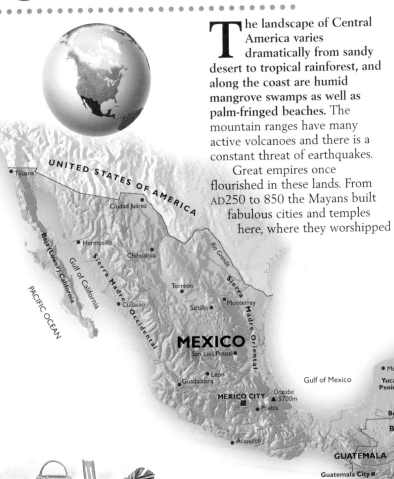

The landscape of Central America varies dramatically from sandy desert to tropical rainforest, and along the coast are humid mangrove swamps as well as palm-fringed beaches. The mountain ranges have many active volcanoes and there is a constant threat of earthquakes.

Great empires once flourished in these lands. From AD250 to 850 the Mayans built fabulous cities and temples here, where they worshipped

Mexican market

Stall-holders prepare for a market in Oaxaca. Mexican farmers were among the first in the world to grow maize, tomatoes, avocados and peppers.

the Caribbean

the Sun and the Moon. In the 1400s the powerful Aztec civilization stretched from coast to coast. Then in 1519 Spanish conquerors came, killing the Aztec rulers and plundering their gold. Central America remained under Spanish control for about 300 years before independence. Most people in Central America are *mestizos*, a mixture of Spanish and Native American, and Spanish is still spoken, along with English and Native American languages.

Havana cigars
● ● ● ● ● ● ● ● ● ● ● ●

A worker hand-rolls a Havana cigar, Cuba's most famous export. The best cigar tobacco comes from plantations in the northwest.

N

BAHAMAS
Nassau ■

TURKS AND CAICOS ISLANDS (U.K.)

Straits of Florida   ATLANTIC OCEAN

ANTIGUA & BARBUDA

Havana ■

CUBA

● Camagüey

DOMINICAN REPUBLIC

San Juan

ST. KITTS AND NEVIS   GUADELOUPE (Fr.)

HAITI
Port-au-Prince ■   ■ Santo Domingo

PUERTO RICO (U.S.A.)   DOMINICA   MARTINIQUE (Fr.)

JAMAICA

ST. LUCIA

CAYMAN ISLANDS (U.K.)   Kingston   ST. VINCENT   BARBADOS

GRENADA

CARIBBEAN SEA

NETHERLANDS ANTILLES

TRINIDAD AND TOBAGO

DURAS

igalpa

CARAGUA

anagua

Panama Canal   Panama City

■ San José

COSTA RICA   PANAMA

COLOMBIA

0 100 200 300 400 500 600 700 800 Kilometres
0   100   200   300   400   500 Miles

Black howler monkey
● ● ● ● ● ● ● ● ●

The black howler monkey is found in Belize. It is at risk because the loss of forests is threatening its habitat.

35

Antigua &
Barbuda

Bahamas

Cuba

Dominican
Republic

Dominica

■ **MEXICO**
Area: 1,967,180 sq km
Population: 91,261,000
Capital: Mexico City
(15,048,000)
Official language:
Spanish
Currency: Mexican peso
Main exports: Petroleum
and petroleum products,
vehicles, engines, cotton,
machinery, coffee, fish,
fertilizers, minerals

■ **PANAMA**
Area: 77,080 sq km
Population: 2,515,000
Capital: Panama City
(585,000)
Official language:
Spanish
Currency: Balboa
Main exports: Bananas,
shrimps, coffee, sugar,
textiles, petroleum
products

■ **TRINIDAD AND
TOBAGO**
Area: 5,130 sq km
Population: 1,260,000
Capital: Port-of-Spain
(59,000)
Official language: English
Currency: Trinidad and
Tobago dollar
Main exports: Petroleum
and petroleum products,
chemicals, rum, sugar

■ **BELIZE**
Area: 22,960 sq km
Population: 205,000
Capital: Belmopan
(5,300)
Official language: English
Currency: Belize dollar
Main exports: Timber,
sugar, fish products,
clothes, fruit

■ **GUATEMALA**
Area: 108,890 sq km
Population: 10,029,000
Capital: Guatemala City
(2,000,000)
Official language:
Spanish
Currency: Quetzal
Main exports: Coffee,
sugar, bananas, cotton,
beef, cardamom

■ **NICARAGUA**
Area: 130,680 sq km
Population: 4,265,000
Capital: Managua
(683,000)
Official language:
Spanish
Currency: Córdoba
Main exports: Coffee,
cotton, sugar,
chemical products,
meat, bananas

■ **ST LUCIA**
Area: 620 sq km
Population: 139,000
Capital: Castries (54,000)
Official language:
English
Currency: East Caribbean
dollar
Main exports: Bananas,
coconuts, cocoa

■ **BAHAMAS**
Area: 13,860 sq km
Population: 269,000
Capital: Nassau
(136,000)
Official language: English
Currency: Bahamian
dollar
Main exports: Mineral
fuels, chemicals, cement,
crayfish, rum

■ **HAITI**
Area: 27,750 sq km
Population: 6,903,000
Capital: Port-au-Prince
(1,402,000)
Official languages:
French, Creole
Currency: Gourde
Main exports: Assembled
goods, coffee, sugar, sisal

■ **HONDURAS**
Area: 112,090 sq km
Population: 5,595,000
Capital: Tegucigalpa
(679,000)
Official language:
Spanish
Currency: Lempira
Main exports: Coffee,
bananas, timber,
meat, sugar, shrimps,
lobsters

■ **JAMAICA**
Area: 11,430 sq km
Population: 2,495,000
Capital: Kingston
(588,000)
Official language: English
Currency: Jamaican dollar
Main exports: Sugar,
bauxite, alumina,
bananas, fruit

St Lucia

Haiti

Jamaica

Belize

El Salvador

Honduras

Barbados

Grenada

St Christopher
(Kitts)-Nevis

St Vincent &
Grenadines

Trinidad &
Tobago

■ CUBA
Area: 110,860 sq km
Population: 10,905,000
Capital: Havana
(2,015,000)
Official language:
Spanish
Currency: Cuban peso
Main exports: Sugar,
minerals, fruit, fish,
coffee

■ DOMINICA
Area: 750 sq km
Population: 72,000
Capital: Roseau (9,000)
Official language:
English
Currency: East Caribbean
dollar
Main exports: Bananas,
coconuts, fruit juices,
essential oils

■ GRENADA
Area: 345 sq km
Population: 92,000
Capital: St George's
(36,000)
Official language: English
Currency: East Caribbean
dollar
Main exports: Nutmeg,
cocoa, bananas

■ PUERTO RICO
Area: 8,900 sq km
Population: 3,620,000
Capital: San Juan
(438,000)
Official language:
Spanish
Currency: US dollar
Main exports: Sugar,
coffee, chemicals,
electronic equipment

■ BARBADOS
Area: 430 sq km
Population: 260,000
Capital: Bridgetown
(7,000)
Official language:
English
Currency: Barbados dollar
Main exports: Sugar,
chemicals, clothes,
electronic equipment

■ DOMINICAN
REPUBLIC
Area: 48,440 sq km
Population: 7,608,000
Capital: Santo Domingo
(1,314,000)
Official language:
Spanish
Currency: Peso
Main exports: Sugar,
molasses, ferro-nickel,
gold, cocoa, coffee

■ ST KITTS-NEVIS
Area: 260 sq km
Population: 42,000
Capital: Basseterre
(15,000)
Official language: English
Currency: East Caribbean
dollar
Main exports: Sugar,
cotton, electronics

■ ST VINCENT AND
THE GRENADINES
Area: 390 sq km
Population: 111,000
Capital: Kingstown
(27,000)
Official language: English
Currency: East Caribbean
dollar
Main export: Bananas

■ ANTIGUA AND
BARBUDA
Area: 440 sq km
Population: 67,000
Capital: St John's
(30,000)
Official language: English
Currency: East Caribbean
dollar
Main exports: Cotton,
sugar, fruit, clothes,
manufactured goods

■ COSTA RICA
Area: 51,100 sq km
Population: 3,199,000
Capital: San José
(297,000)
Official language:
Spanish
Currency: Costa Rican
colón
Main exports: Coffee,
textiles, bananas, sugar,
cocoa

■ EL SALVADOR
Area: 21,040 sq km
Population: 5,517,000
Capital: San Salvador
(1,523,000)
Official language:
Spanish
Currency: El Salvador
colón
Main exports: Coffee,
sugarcane, shrimps,
flowers, textiles, maize,
cotton

Nicaragua

Mexico

Panama

Puerto Rico

Guatemala

Costa Rica

Mexico

The powerful Aztec civilization flourished in Mexico from the mid-1400s with its capital at Tenochtitlán (now Mexico City). In 1519 Spanish conquerors started a bloody war in the Gulf of Mexico. They defeated the Aztecs, and Spain ruled for the next 300 years. Mexico became independent in 1821, but war with the USA followed and Mexico lost much of its land. This troubled period ended in 1917 and a new system of laws was adopted. Now most Mexicans live in large cities where influences from the USA and Europe are transforming everyday life. However, many people in the villages still speak one of the Native American languages as well as Spanish and the whole country keeps alive festivals that are 5,000 years old.

Fishing in Mexico

These fishermen on Mexico's Lake Patzcuaro are using butterfly nets. They make their boats look as if they had wings.

Nicaragua

Nicaragua gained independence from Spain in 1821. Civil war then divided the country for nearly a century. In 1912 troops from the USA became involved and stayed for 20 years. The military leader, Anastasio Somoza, gained control in 1936. His family ruled as dictators until 1979, when left-wing rebels called Sandinistas took over. Groups known as the contras (which means against) disagreed with the Sandinistas over how the country should be run and fought them, supported by the USA. The Sandinistas were defeated in the 1990 elections and the war ended. Today most Nicaraguans work on small farms or large plantations. Rich landowners established the plantations, but the government now owns many of them.

Coffee

Coffee is an important crop in Central America and the Caribbean. It thrives in the cool foothills of the mountains.

Ripe berries

Roasted beans

Coffee plant

Mexican dancers

At Veracruz dancers called voledores (fliers) perform acrobatics on top of a swinging pole. They are taking part in a traditional festival.

The Caribbean

The West Indies are an island chain that stretches round the Caribbean Sea. They are made up of the Bahamas, the Lesser Antilles and the Greater Antilles (Cuba, Hispaniola and Puerto Rico). Hispaniola is divided into two countries, Haiti and the Dominican Republic.

The islands of the Caribbean are rocky, fringed with coral reefs and covered with tropical forests. Most islanders are descendants of slaves who were brought from Africa to work on plantations growing bananas, sugarcane and spices. The rest are of European, Indian, Chinese or mixed descent.

Tobago

Tobago's white beaches attract many tourists. The warm Caribbean Sea is ideal for sailing, swimming and snorkelling.

The Panama Canal

This important shipping route links the Atlantic and Pacific. It has made Panama City an international finance centre.

Economy

The tropical climate is ideal for growing sugarcane, tobacco, fruit, cotton and coffee. These nations used to depend on farming and fishing for their income. However, since the discovery of oil in the Gulf of Mexico, more people are leaving the countryside to work in mining and other industries. Often they have to live in shanty towns because the cities are not growing fast enough to house them. Another important industry is tourism. Visitors come to enjoy the Caribbean beaches and relaxed way of life.

SOUTH AMERICA

South America has landscapes of immense variety. The hot dusty grasslands of the southern Pampas are cattle-ranching country. In the west, coffee grows in the cool valleys of the high Andes Mountains. The Atacama Desert is one of the driest places in the world. The basin of the mighty Amazon River is covered with dense rainforest, one of the last great wildernesses on Earth.

The diverse Indian cultures developed brilliant civilizations. The last of them were destroyed in the 1500s by conquerors from Spain. As European settlers flooded to the continent, many Indian tribes were wiped out by disease. In the 1820s the settlers began to break away from their European rulers in bloody wars of independence.

Many of the new nations prospered, but usually the settlers grew rich while the Indians stayed poor. Poverty led to strikes and riots and in most countries the military seized power. Over recent decades more democratic governments have been elected. There have been efforts to preserve political stability and improve living standards. The continent has a wealth of natural resources, but earning money from them often upsets the delicate balance of nature.

Kamayura

The Kamayura are just one of the many native peoples living in the rainforests. The men wear earrings and brightly coloured feather headdresses.

Gauchos

A gaucho – a skilled Argentine cowboy – wields his lasso. Gauchos wear high boots with spurs, felt hats and baggy trousers.

■ SOUTH AMERICA FACTS
Area: 17,600,000 sq km
Population: 316,000,000
Independent countries: 12
Highest point: Mt Aconcagua
(6,960 m)
Longest rivers: Amazon (6,448 km),
Rio de la Plata-Parana (4,000 km)
Highest waterfall: Angel Falls (979 m)
Largest lake: Maracaibo
(13,512 sq km)

The Iguaçu Falls

. . . .

The Iguaçu Falls are a string of 275 spectacular waterfalls on the border between Argentina and Brazil. The water cascades down drops of up to 70 m.

Scarlet macaw

. . . .

The scarlet macaw is the brightest of the parrot family. Macaws live in the high canopies of rainforest trees and crack nuts with their powerful beaks.

The Andean States

Colombia, Ecuador, Peru and Bolivia are dominated by the towering peaks of the Andes. Many of these mountains are active volcanoes that occasionally erupt. Moving plates deep under the earth also pose the threat of earthquakes.

The Andes was the homeland of the Incas, who ruled a rich and civilized empire here until the Spanish conquest 600 years ago. Descendants of the Incas still farm the ancient terraced fields on steep mountain ridges, growing potatoes and tomatoes, the original crops of South America. The mountains are also mined for their rich deposits of emeralds, gold and tin, and in Colombia some farmers hide secret crops of the illegal and highly profitable drug cocaine.

Dense tropical rainforest spreads east of the Andes to the heart of the continent. Valuable deposits of oil have been found here, endangering the future of the forest, its animals and Native American inhabitants.

Cathedral in Ecuador

This Roman Catholic cathedral is in Cuenca, a city founded by Spanish conquerors in 1557. Christianity is the official religion in the Andean states.

Way of life

Most people of the Andean states live in modern cities. They work in mines that yield emeralds or coal, or in factories that produce a wide range of goods, from steel to cement or clothing. The high-rise buildings of the city centres are often surrounded by large suburbs of shanty towns where the poorer people live. Some people lead a more traditional life as farmers in mountain villages. They often supplement their income by producing crafts to sell to tourists. Only a few groups,

Boat people

The Uru people, living on Lake Titicaca in Peru, travel in boats made of reeds. They also use reeds to make their houses, which are built on rafts of reeds floating on the lake.

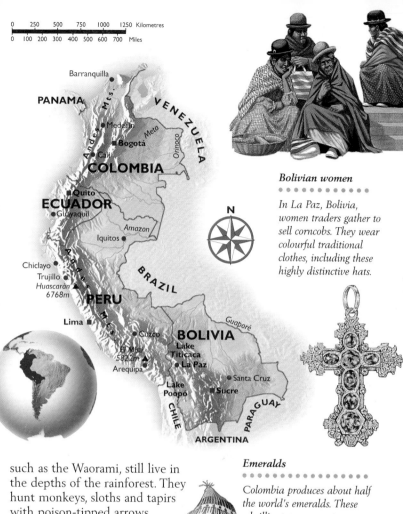

Bolivian women
. . . .

In La Paz, Bolivia, women traders gather to sell corncobs. They wear colourful traditional clothes, including these highly distinctive hats.

such as the Waorami, still live in the depths of the rainforest. They hunt monkeys, sloths and tapirs with poison-tipped arrows. They clear land to build villages of thatched huts, grow small amounts of crops, then move on after harvest to hunt and fish. Many Native Americans speak their own languages, such as Quechua, but Spanish is the official language of the Andean States.

Emeralds
. . . .

Colombia produces about half the world's emeralds. These brilliant green gemstones are often set in Colombian gold to make valuable jewellery.

Peruvian musician
. . . .

A Native American musician, wearing a traditional hat and cape, plays a haunting tune on the pan-pipes.

43

Farming and fishing

On the steamy coastal plains west of the Andes, the climate is ideal for growing cotton, bananas, cocoa and sugarcane. Abundant rain falls in the mountains, and it is cooler there. A wide range of crops, including coffee, is grown on the fertile hillsides. There are cattle farms on the lush rolling grasslands and northern plains. Fishing is another major source of income. The Pacific yields large catches of herring and tuna.

La Paz, Bolivia

* * * * * * * * * *

Skyscrapers tower against a backdrop of mountains in Bolivia's financial and administrative capital, La Paz. The country's legal capital is Sucre.

Bolivian trader

* * * * * * * * * *

This man is selling traditional shawls and blankets. Native Americans make these woollens for their own use as well as to sell to tourists.

Inca civilization

The original inhabitants of the Andean States were Native American peoples. The most brilliant of these were the Incas, who came to power in the 1400s. They followed the Huari and the Chimu peoples in a series of civilizations that first developed in Peru about 3,000 years ago. The Inca period was famous for its monumental architecture and for beautifully crafted gold and pottery. The Incas used precious metals freely because they were readily available. Careful organization and a good network of roads enabled them to hold together a vast empire that covered all the central Andes.

Spanish conquest

In 1532 the conqueror Francisco Pizarro arrived from Spain in search of treasure, and set about killing the Incas and destroying their empire. During the 300 years that Spain ruled the Andean states, thousands of Spanish

Oil workers in Ecuador

* * * * * * * * * *

Workers drill for oil in the remote eastern rainforests on the border with Peru. Both Ecuador and Peru lay claim to this region, intending to exploit its valuable resources.

settlers arrived. They brought slaves from Africa to work alongside Native American survivors on sugarcane plantations. Many groups of Native Americans were destroyed or killed by disease. Only a few of the original communities still lead traditional lifestyles today.

Independence

In the early 1800s the Andean States won their independence from Spain in a series of bloody battles. But independence did not win peace, and political unrest is never far from the surface in these countries today. A deep cultural and economic division still exists between the Native Americans and the descendants of the Spanish settlers.

Peruvian dagger

Dating back some 700 years to the Chimu period, this ornate dagger is shaped like a man. It is made of gold and studded with the semi-precious stone turquoise.

El Dorado

This gold model shows El Dorado (The Golden Man) on his raft. Legendary tales of this rich king drew Spanish conquerors in search of gold.

■ **COLOMBIA**
Area: 1,141,750 sq km
Population: 33,951,000
Capital: Bogotá (4,922,000)
Official language: Spanish
Currency: Colombian peso
Main exports: Coffee, emeralds, petroleum, coal, flowers, meat

■ **ECUADOR**
Area: 283,560 sq km (Galapagos Islands 7,844 sq km)
Population: 10,981,000
Capital: Quito (1,101,000)
Official language: Spanish
Currency: Sucre
Main exports: Bananas, petroleum, shrimps, coffee, cocoa, sugar

■ **PERU**
Area: 1,244,280 sq km
Population: 22,454,000
Capital: Lima (5,760,000)
Official languages: Spanish, Quechua
Currency: New sol
Main exports: Copper, lead, fish products, iron, zinc, oil, coffee, llama and alpaca wool, cotton, sugar

■ **BOLIVIA**
Area: 1,098,580 sq km
Population: 7,065,000
Capitals: Sucre (106,000), La Paz (670,000)
Official language: Spanish
Currency: Boliviano
Main exports: Natural gas, oil, tin, zinc, silver, gold, coffee, sugar

Colombia

Ecuador

Peru

Bolivia

Brazil and

its neighbours

Caribbean Sea

TRINIDAD
AND TOBAGO

Caracas

Maracaibo

COLOMBIA

Orinoco

VENEZUELA

Georgetown

Paramaribo

GUYANA

Cayenne

Orinoco

Guiana Highlands

SURINAM

FRENCH
GUIANA

ATLANTIC
OCEAN

Branco

Negro

Japurá

Macapá

Manaus

Amazon

Belém

Amazon

Tocantins

Juruá

Purus

Madeira

Tapajós

Xingu

Fortale

Guaporé

PERU

BOLIVIA

Araguaia

Parnaíba

São Francisco

Rec

BRAZIL

Brazilian
Highlands

Salvador

Mato Grosso
Plateau

BRASÍLIA

Goiânia

PARAGUAY

Belo Horizonte

Paraná

Rio de Janeiro

São Paulo

Iguaçu
Falls

Curitiba

ARGENTINA

Uruguay

URUGUAY

Pôrto Alegre

N

Simón Bolívar

*This statue in Caracas, Venezuela,
commemorates Simón Bolívar. He
led the revolution against Spanish
rule in the early 1800s.*

Brazil is full of natural wonders. The brown sluggish waters of the mighty Amazon River snake their way through the world's largest area of dense rainforest. The forest spreads into Guyana, Surinam and French Guiana and is known only to the Native Americans who hunt and fish there, their lives barely touched by the modern world.

Brazil also has rich mineral resources and fertile soils that produce coffee, cocoa and sugarcane. Every year Brazilians celebrate the most famous carnival in the world, which has its centre at Rio de Janeiro. This city shows the huge gap between rich and poor in Brazil, with modern high-rise buildings surrounded by slums.

The country has serious economic problems. Huge areas of the Amazon rainforest are being destroyed to make new farmland and grazing land, which means that rare animals and medicinal plants are lost forever. This has become an environmental issue of worldwide concern.

Space station, French Guiana
● ● ● ● ● ● ● ● ● ● ● ● ● ● ● ● ● ●

An Ariane rocket stands in the Assembly Hall of the European Space Agency station at Kourou. Rockets launched from this station on the coast of French Guiana often carry satellites into space.

Brazil nuts
● ● ● ● ● ● ● ● ● ● ● ● ● ● ● ● ● ●

Many Brazil nut trees in the Amazon rainforest are being cut down to make farmland that will yield less nutritious crops from the same amount of land.

Piranha fish
● ● ● ● ● ● ● ● ● ● ●

Meat-eating piranha fish have very sharp teeth. If a wounded animal falls into the Amazon River they strip its flesh in minutes.

Chillies
● ● ● ● ● ● ● ● ● ● ●

Red and green chilli peppers are dried and ground to make cayenne pepper. This fiery spice is named after the capital of French Guiana, Cayenne.

47

Industry and agriculture

Brazil is South America's leading industrial nation and the world's largest producer of coffee and sugarcane. There are enormous reserves of iron ore here and the country's mines also yield gold and diamonds. Large deposits of oil have been found in the Amazon basin.

Venezuela is the richest nation in South America, due to valuable reserves of oil discovered in Lake Maracaibo. Oil exports earn about three-quarters of Venezuela's income. Industry is centred in cities on the coastal strip, where products range from cars to medicines. Venezuela also has valuable deposits of bauxite and manganese and thriving new aluminium and steel works.

Carnival

• • • • • • • • • •

Carnival-goers celebrate in Brazil. Carnival is a five-day party that marks the start of Lent, 40 days before Easter.

History

During the 1500s Europeans invaded South America, drawn by the lure of gold. They killed many Native Americans and forced others into slavery. Brazil was ruled by the Portuguese, Venezuela by the Spanish, Guyana by the British and Surinam by the Dutch. Independence came to most of the continent in the 1800s, but French Guiana is still a dependency of France and receives aid from the French government.

Forest products

Guyana is one of the world's biggest producers of bauxite, and also has deposits of manganese and gold. Like its neighbour Surinam, it grows sugarcane and bananas. Cutting valuable timber for export in the countries of the Amazon Basin has driven Native Americans deeper into the rainforests.

Surinam horse dance

• • • • • • • • • • • • • • • •

Descendants of the Javanese people who came to live in Surinam keep their heritage alive by performing a traditional dance.

Cathedral in Brasilia
● ●

Imposing sculptures line the route to the spectacular modern cathedral in Brasilia, the capital city of Brazil.

Rainforest wildlife

South America has one of the richest varieties of wildlife in the world. In the Amazon basin alone there are at least 44,000 different kinds of plants, 2,500 types of river fish and 1,500 species of birds. In the rainforest there are large bird-eating spiders and mammals include armadillos, jaguars and sloths. In the rivers are manatees, freshwater dolphins, giant catfish and electric eels. Of the thousands of forest insects, many have yet to be identified and studied.

Hallacas
● ● ● ● ● ● ● ● ● ● ● ● ●

Hallacas is a Venezuelan Christmas pasty of meat in maize flour pastry. It is eaten with bread and ham (right).

■ **VENEZUELA**
Area: 912,050 sq km
Population: 20,712,000
Capital: Caracas (1,045,000)
Official language: Spanish
Currency: Bolivar
Main exports: Coffee, oil, iron ore, textiles, fruit, aluminium

■ **GUYANA**
Area: 214,970 sq km
Population: 816,000
Capital: Georgetown (188,000)
Official language: English
Currency: Guyana dollar
Main exports: Gold, aluminium, sugar, rice, rum, bauxite, timber

■ **SURINAM**
Area: 163,820 sq km
Population: 446,000
Capital: Paramaribo (201,000)
Official language: Dutch
Currency: Surinam guilder
Main exports: Alumina, bauxite, aluminium, shrimps, rice, bananas, timber

■ **FRENCH GUIANA**
Area: 83,530 sq km
Population: 108,000
Capital: Cayenne (42,000)
Official language: French
Currency: French franc
Main exports: Shrimps, prawns, rice, timber and metal products

■ **BRAZIL**
Area: 8,512,000 sq km
Population: 159,143,000
Capital: Brasilia (1,597,000)
Official language: Portuguese
Currency: Real
Main exports: Iron ore, coffee, fruit, timber, sugar, vehicles, beef

Guyana

Surinam

French Guiana

Brazil

49

The Southern States

0 25 50 75 100 Kilometres
0 10 20 30 40 50 60 70 Miles

PERU

Arica
Iquique

BOLIVIA

Antofagasta

CHILE

PARAGUAY

Gran
Chaco

BRAZIL

Asunción

Tucumán

Salado

Paraná

Uruguay

ARGENTINA

Córdoba

Rosario

URUGUAY

Montevideo

Valparaíso
Santiago

Aconcagua
6959m

BUENOS AIRES

Concepción

Pampas

Mar del
Plata

Colorado

Bahía
Blanca

Negro

N

Andes

Chubut

PATAGONIA

Paraguayan lace

A Paraguayan lacemaker works
at a bedspread in traditional
Guaraní (Native American)
style. Flowers, birds, animals and
decorative patterns are created
out of the lace, which is called
ñandutí, the Guaraní word for
spider's web.

FALKLAND ISLANDS (U.K.)

Tierra del
Fuego

Cape Horn

SOUTH GEORGIA (U.K.)

Seat of government in Argentina

The Congress Building in
Buenos Aires, Argentina's capital
city, is built in the French style.
Buenos Aires is often referred to as
the 'Paris of South America'.
Buenos Aires is the Spanish for
'fair winds' and the city is a major
international port.

Around 500 years ago only Native Americans lived in this region, including the Incas in northern Chile, the Guaraní in the tropical northeast and the Guajira in the far south. Then in the 1500s the Spanish fortune-hunters arrived and began to take control. Gradually the indigenous peoples fell victim to European diseases, died in slavery, or were massacred.

The wars of independence fought with Spain during the early 1800s did not lead to peace. They were followed instead by bitter internal strife, economic crises and periods of military rule. In recent decades the Southern States have become democratically elected republics.

Most of the people of this region are of European or mixed descent. Native Americans form only a small minority. Immigrants continue to flood into prosperous Argentina. It is proud of being a multicultural land, with a population including British, Hungarians, Italians and Lebanese. All keep alive their national customs and traditions.

Steam train

This steam train is used to transport tropical hardwood across Paraguay. The timber is a valuable resource, but its harvest is wiping out large tracts of rainforest.

Montevideo, Uruguay

A statue in Uruguay's capital celebrates the early Spanish settlers. They crossed the country with ox-drawn carts to build towns and farms inland.

Spectacular landscapes

Chile is the longest, thinnest country in the world. The fertile central area is occupied by wheatfields and orchards. To the north lies the arid Atacama Desert. The far south is a land of forests, mountains and glaciers. Oil and natural gas have been found among the southern islands, and the country is also rich in minerals. Most Chileans live in the coastal cities and work in industry. Chile and Argentina are divided by the majestic Andes Mountains.

Beef country

The Spanish gave Argentina its name. They believed they would find rich deposits of silver here and called the land after *argentum*, the Latin word for silver. As it turned out, they were proved wrong. Argentina's greatest treasure is its lush pastureland and fertile soil, which stretches across into Uruguay and eastern Paraguay.

Argentina's economy was founded on the meat and leather industry in the 1800s. Its best grazing land is the Pampas, rolling plains where cowboys called gauchos herd prime beef cattle. Much of the Pampas is divided into huge *estancias* (ranches) owned by a wealthy few.

In the warm foothills of the Andes is a rich farming area, producing wheat, oranges and grapes. The west of Paraguay and Argentina's far northwest are known as the Gran Chaco, an area of bleak salt marshes. To the south lies Patagonia, a scrubby land that bakes in summer and freezes in winter. Most people here are sheep farmers.

Maté tea-drinker
● ●

This man sips maté tea from a gourd, through a metal tube. Maté is a hot bitter tea drunk all over South America.

■ **CHILE**
Area: 736,900 sq km
Population: 13,813,000
Capital: Santiago (4,859,000)
Official language: Spanish
Currency: Chilean peso
Main exports: Copper, iron, fruit, wood pulp

■ **PARAGUAY**
Area: 406,750 sq km
Population: 4,643,000
Capital: Asunción (945,000)
Official language: Spanish
Currency: Guaraní
Main exports: Cotton, soya beans, timber, meat, vegetable oil

■ **URUGUAY**
Area: 176,210 sq km
Population: 3,149,000
Capital: Montevideo (1,384,000)
Official language: Spanish
Currency: Uruguayan peso
Main exports: Meat, leather, hides, wool, fish, textiles

■ **ARGENTINA**
Area: 2,870,092 sq km
Population: 33,778,000
Capital: Buenos Aires (9,928,000)
Official language: Spanish
Currency: Peso
Main exports: Wheat, maize, meat, hides, wool, tannin, linseed oil

Chile

Paraguay

Uruguay

Argentina

Valuable tourist trade

The majority of Uruguayans live along the south coast, which overlooks the wide estuary of the Río de la Plata (Plate River) and the Atlantic Ocean. In summer large numbers of tourists flock to the sandy beaches of this long coastline. Just inland begin fertile, low-lying plains, where crops such as rice, tangerines, peaches and grapes grow through the hot summers and mild winters, watered by regular rainfall.

Beyond the plains lie rich pastures with huge farms that raise cattle and sheep. Leather, wool and meat products are a vital source of income to Uruguay. A great deal of meat is eaten in the country and beef is Uruguay's favourite meal.

Parliament in Paraguay

The Paraguay National Congress Parliament Building stands in the nation's capital, Asunción. The city was founded in the 1500s by Spanish conquerors on their way to seek gold in Peru.

Fertile farmlands

Landlocked Paraguay is a hot and humid country, divided in two by the Paraguay River. To the east are lush grasslands and thick forests. Almost all Paraguayans live here, mainly ranching cattle and farming sugarcane, rice, coffee and soya beans. To the west the Gran Chaco is a vast plain of salt marshes, thorny scrub and sparse grass. Paraguay remains a poor country, but its fertile farmlands and potential for hydro-electric power promise a brighter future.

Chilean copper mine

Chuquicamata in northern Chile is one of the largest open-cast copper mines in the world. Copper is Chile's main export.

A ruined church in Argentina

These ruins at San Ignacio are a legacy of the Jesuits, who came to the region in the 1600s to convert the Guarani peoples.

EUROPE

Throughout its history Europe has greatly influenced world politics. The ancient Greeks invented democracy in about 450BC. This system, where the government is chosen by the people, is widespread today. By the 1700s Europeans were practising colonialism. Powerful seafaring nations such as Spain, the Netherlands and Britain ruled much of the world. They grew rich from exploiting Asia, Africa and the Americas. Many of these colonies did not gain their independence until this century.

London's Buckingham Palace

Buckingham Palace, at the heart of Britain's capital, London, is the official residence of the royal family. Today European kings and queens have limited powers.

Both World Wars began in Europe. After World War II (1939–1945) the continent split into communist countries in the east, led by the Soviet Union, and non-communist countries in the west, supported by the USA. Europe became the centre of a power struggle between the two sides known as the Cold War. The Cold War ended with the collapse of communism in the 1980s and 1990s, but conflict between ethnic groups and economic problems caused new tensions in eastern Europe.

By 1996, 15 western European nations had joined the European Union. This organization works to unite the different countries of Europe politically and economically.

■ CONTINENTAL FACTS

Area: 10,539,000 sq km
(including the European parts of Russia and Turkey)
Population: 584,000,000
(excluding Russia)
Independent countries: 44
(excluding Russia and Turkey)
Largest country: Russia
(about 25% of Russia is in Europe; 75% in Asia)
Smallest country: Vatican City
Highest point: Mt Elbrus, Russia
(5,633 m)
Largest lake: Caspian Sea
(360,700 sq km, partly in Europe, partly in Asia)
Longest river: Volga (3,690 km)

Spanish oranges

Spain, in sunny southern Europe, is one of the world's largest exporters of citrus fruits. Bitter oranges from Seville are made into marmalade.

European Union

The flags of the European Union fly outside the Council of Europe in Strasbourg, France. The European Union was set up in the 1950s. It has grown since then and today has 15 member nations. Its object is to unify European politics and economics.

Hedgehog

The hedgehog is a nocturnal animal that rolls up into a ball when attacked. Its fur has evolved into spines that keep enemies at bay. Hedgehogs hibernate in their nests over winter.

Scandinavia and Finland

Isafjördur
Vatneyri
Hólmavík
Bordeyri
Húsavik
Saudárkrókur
Akureyri
Seydisfjördur
ICELAND
Vatnajökull
Akranes
REYKJAVIK
Keflavík
▲ Oraefajökull
2119m
Vestmannaeyjar

Scandinavia and Finland are among the northernmost inhabited areas of the world. Northern Scandinavia lies inside the Arctic Circle, and is called the Land of the Midnight Sun, because it is light for 24 hours a day around midsummer and dark for much of the day in December. While the north of this area has an Arctic climate, the south is kept mild by the Gulf Stream, a warm ocean current.

The rugged scenery of these northern countries is the legacy of the last Ice Age. The ice caps and glaciers are the remains of a huge sheet of ice that covered much of northern Europe 10,000 years ago. In Norway the glaciers gouged out steep valleys and sea inlets called fiords, deep enough to carry ocean-going ships. In Finland and Sweden the ice ground out thousands of lakes, and dotted the lakes and the coastline with tiny islands. The southernmost country of the group, Denmark, has a low-lying mainland and nearly 500 islands. Its territory includes two self-governing protectorates, the windswept Faeroes and the vast Arctic wastes of Greenland, which is on the other side of the Atlantic Ocean east of Canada.

The island of Iceland is known as the Land of Ice and Fire because it has active volcanoes and geysers set in a dramatic landscape of icefields and glaciers. As recently as 1963 a volcano under the sea created a new offshore island, Surtsey, as lava bubbled up from the ocean floor.

Åles

B

Sta

Fish processing

Fish are sorted at a processing plant in Tromsø. The catch of herring, whiting, cod and haddock is frozen and canned as well as dried in the traditional way.

N

ARCTIC OCEAN

Hammerfest
Vadsø
Kirkenes

NORTH ATLANTIC
OCEAN

Tromsø
▲ Mount Haltia
1324m

L a p l a n d

Narvik
Kebnekaise
▲ 2111m

Svolvær

Sodankylä

Kiruna

Bodø

Rovaniemi

Övertorneå

Mosjøen

Kemi

Storuman
Skellefte
Ume

Luleå

Skellefteå

Oulu

SWEDEN
Umeå

Kokkola

Kuopio

RUSSIA

Trondheim
Östersund

Vaasa

Joensuu

stiansund

Kaskö
Jyväskylä

dhopiggen
2469m

Sundsvall

FINLAND

Särna

Tampere

Lahti

ammer

Västerdal

Turku
HELSINKI

ORWAY

Gävle
**Aland
Is.**

Gulf of Finland

OSLO

Karlstad
Uppsala

ESTONIA

kien

Örebro
STOCKHOLM

Lake
Vänern

ansand

Baltic Sea

Linköping

errak

Göteborg
Borås

Västervik
Gotland

borg

Kattegat

Borgholm

ENMARK

Karlskrona

hus
COPENHAGEN
Kristianstad

Odense
Malmö

Gulf of Bothnia

GERMANY

| 0 | 100 | 200 | 300 | Kilometres |

| 0 | 50 | 100 | 150 | 200 | Miles |

The riches of the sea

In these northern countries, the sea plays an important role in people's lives. Fishing has long been one of the most important industries of Scandinavia, helped by the warm ocean currents that flow in the Atlantic and keep the coasts free of ice. Norwegians have exported dried fish since the early 1200s. Today fish is still dried, as well as frozen and canned. Fleets from Iceland, Norway, and Denmark trawl the North Atlantic and Greenland Sea in search of cod, herring, capelin and haddock. Shipbuilding is another major industry. The shipyards of Finland specialize in icebreakers and ferries that cross the rough northern waters. Since oil was discovered in the North Sea in the early 1960s, the Norwegians have become expert at constructing oil rigs as well as building fishing vessels in their many natural harbours.

■ NORWAY
Area: 386,960 sq km
Population: 4,312,000
Capital: Oslo (460,000)
Official language: Norwegian
Currency: Norwegian krone
Main exports: Oil and oil products, natural gas, ships, fish, paper, wood pulp, machinery

■ SWEDEN
Area: 449,960 sq km
Population: 8,716,000
Capital: Stockholm (685,000)
Official language: Swedish
Currency: Krona
Main exports: Vehicles, machinery, iron, steel, paper products

■ FINLAND
Area: 338,150 sq km
Population: 5,067,000
Capital: Helsinki (502,000)
Official languages: Finnish, Swedish
Currency: Euro, Markka
Main exports: Timber, vehicles, paper products, machinery, ships, clothes, furniture

■ DENMARK
Area: 43,080 sq km
Population: 5,189,000
Capital: Copenhagen (1,343,000)
Official language: Danish
Currency: Danish krone
Main exports: Meat, fish, dairy products, electrical equipment, machinery, transport equipment

■ ICELAND
Area: 103,000 sq km
Population: 263,000
Capital: Reykjavik (101,000)
Official language: Icelandic
Currency: Krona
Main exports: Fish and fish products, shellfish, crustaceans, animal feed, aluminium, iron, steel, diatomite

Sami people in Lapland
● ●

Today only a small number of Sami (Lapp) people live the traditional nomadic way of life, keeping reindeer for their meat, milk, and hides.

Swedish ski school

. . . .

In Sweden children old enough to walk are ready to learn to ski. Skiing is a useful way of getting about and a popular sport.

Natural resources

The prosperity of these modern nations is built on the development of their natural resources. Oil and gas are drilled in the North Sea. The Danes have developed wind turbines to harness wind power and generate electricity. Rivers in Sweden and Finland are dammed to produce hydro-electric power. Dense forests provide plentiful timber for furniture and paper-making. To ensure future supplies of timber and protect the environment, forests are continually replanted.

Volcanic rocks

. . . .

Black rocks rise from the waters of Lake Myvatn in Iceland. They were formed from the cooled lava of ancient volcanoes.

The Scandinavian people

The people of Scandinavia share a common history. In the early Middle Ages they were Vikings, the seafarers and warriors who sailed to Iceland, Greenland and North America. They also raided and settled in parts of Russia and northern Europe.

The earliest known people to settle in Scandinavia were the Sami (Lapps). Their descendants still live in Lapland, north of the Arctic Circle. Some Sami lead the traditional nomadic way of life, herding reindeer and fishing. Others work in factories or mines.

These five northern nations are peaceful and prosperous and enjoy some of the best standards of living in the world. People pay high taxes, but have many welfare benefits, including free healthcare, education, and pensions.

Danish pastries

. . . .

These sweet rolls are rich, flaky, and often iced. The Danes eat them with coffee at any time of the day.

Netherlands, Belgium and Luxembourg

The Netherlands, Belgium and Luxembourg form a region known as the Low Countries. By the 1300s the French dukes of Burgundy were in control of this area. In the early 1500s the Low Countries joined the immense empire of the Habsburg family, whose lands included Spain and Austria. The region grew rich through trade. Then many people in the Low Countries joined the Protestant religion introduced from neighbouring Germany. They resented being ruled by Spain, a Roman Catholic country, and rebelled against the Habsburgs. After many battles they shook off Spanish power in 1648.

During the 1600s the Netherlands became one of the world's leading seafaring nations and acquired a large overseas empire.

Dutch cheese

Round, wax-covered cheeses are carried on sleds to market in Alkmaar, a popular destination for tourists. The Netherlands exports large amounts of cheese to countries all over the world.

Trade with the Dutch East Indies (Indonesia) brought great wealth to the Netherlands. At the end of the 1600s Dutch power began to decline. Belgium broke away to become a separate nation in 1830, followed by Luxembourg in 1867. In this century the three countries have rebuilt close links and prospered. In 1948 they forged an economic union known as Benelux. In 1957 they were founder members of the European Union.

Belgian carnival

Belgians dress up as giants for an annual parade around town streets. The costumes have peep-holes in their skirts so the people hidden inside can see where they are going.

Grape harvest
● ● ● ● ● ● ● ● ● ● ● ●

*Harvesters tip grapes
into a vat to begin
making Moselle wine.
The grapes are grown
on Luxembourg's steep
terraced hillsides by the
Moselle River.*

| 0 | 25 | 50 | 75 | 100 | Kilometres |
| 0 | 10 | 20 | 30 | 40 | 50 | 60 | Miles |

West Frisian Islands

Waddenzee

Leeuwarden   Groningen ●

IJsselmeer

AMSTERDAM ■

                                    Enschede ●

● Leiden   **NETHERLANDS**
● The Hague

              Lek   ● Arnhem

● Rotterdam

        Maas   Nijmegen ●

    ● Breda   ● Tilburg
                    ● Eindhoven

● Ostend   ● Antwerp   GERMANY
  Bruges   Ghent ●

      Leie   ● Maastricht
        Schelde   ■ **BRUSSELS**

        BELGIUM   ● Liège

    ● Mons   ● Namur   Meuse   Botrange ▲
        ● Charleroi   694m

      Sambre   Ardennes Mts.

FRANCE
                        Bastogne ●

                              LUXEMBOURG

                        ■ **LUXEMBOURG**

N

Economy

The standard of living in these countries is high. Belgium is one of the most heavily industrialized countries in Europe and steel manufacturing is its most important industry. Rich deposits of iron have made Luxembourg another leading steel producer. Its capital, Luxembourg City, is an international centre of banking and finance.

The Netherlands is famous worldwide for its dairy produce, greenhouse vegetables, cut flowers, bulbs and seeds. Dutch factories produce a wide range of goods from electrical appliances to textiles and chemicals.

- **BELGIUM**
  Area: 30,530 sq km
  Population: 10,010,000
  Capital: Brussels (951,000)
  Official languages: Dutch, French
  Currency: Euro, Belgian franc
  Main exports: Iron, steel, machinery, transport equipment, chemicals, processed food, cut diamonds, textiles, plastics

- **NETHERLANDS**
  Area: 41,530 sq km
  Population: 15,287,000
  Capital: Amsterdam (1,092,000)
  Official language: Dutch
  Currency: Euro, Guilder
  Main exports: Dairy produce, flower bulbs, vegetables, petrochemicals, electronic equipment

- **LUXEMBOURG**
  Area: 2,590 sq km
  Population: 380,000
  Capital: Luxembourg City (76,000)
  Official languages: French, German, Letzebuergesch
  Currency: Euro, Luxembourg franc
  Main exports: Iron, steel, textiles, machinery, chemicals, plastics

Geography

The word Netherlands means lowlands. The country is almost entirely flat and much of the land lies below sea level. There are large areas of polder, land that has been drained or reclaimed from the sea. The delta region of the southwest is protected against flooding by a series of huge dams and floodgates.

Flat farmland reclaimed from the sea also forms much of Belgium's coastal lowlands. These rise to fertile plateaus in the centre of the country and to the wooded hills of the Ardennes in the southeast. The Ardennes extend into the north of Luxembourg and the Sauer and Moselle Rivers form its eastern boundary. The south, with its green pastures and fertile farmland, is known as the Bon Pays (Good Land).

Dutch windmills

The Netherlands is famous for tulips and windmills. Wind power was used to drain the land. Today this work is done by modern pumps.

Luxembourg City

The member countries of the European Union fly their flags in a brisk wind outside the Secretariat of the European Parliament in the capital of Luxembourg. Luxembourg City is a major centre of finance and administration.

A carpet of flowers

A carpet of begonias decorates a square in the centre of Brussels, Belgium's capital. This display is created every other August.

Copper butterfly

The copper butterfly lives in Belgium's central lowlands. Numbers are decreasing because of the draining of its marshland habitat.

People

The people who live in the Netherlands are known as the Dutch, and their country is sometimes called Holland. They and their lowland neighbours are mainly descended from Germanic peoples called the Franks, Frisians and Saxons, who settled in this region about 2,000 years ago.

The Belgians are divided into two main ethnic groups. The Dutch-speaking Flemings live in northern Belgium and the French-speaking Walloons in the south. To reduce tensions between the two, Belgium has created separate regions that have considerable control over local matters. The people of Luxembourg speak French, German, and Letzebuergesch. Most people of this region live in cities and work in industry.

Transport

The flat landscape of the Netherlands is cut by a network of rivers, canals and dikes. Barges make their way up and down the waterways. In Belgium, the Meuse and Schelde rivers have been important trade routes for centuries. Goods are also carried across the heavily industrialized lowlands by truck and train. Spreading suburbs and high-rise flats are found in most cities, but city centres have often changed little for centuries. There are fine old brick houses that date back to the 1600s. Cyclists are a common sight as the flat ground makes bicycles the ideal form of personal transport.

63

The British Isles

The British Isles consists of England, Scotland and Wales on the mainland, and the island of Ireland. Northern Ireland belongs with England, Scotland and Wales to the United Kingdom (UK), while the south is the independent Republic of Ireland.

The UK was the first nation in the world to change from an agricultural economy to an industrial one. It has a large population for its size. But outside its crowded towns and cities there is beautiful countryside – the heather-covered glens of Scotland, the deep valleys and mountains of Wales, and the rolling fields of England and Ireland. A mild, wet climate makes much of the land green and fertile.

During the Middle Ages the countries of the British Isles were often at war with one another. From the 1500s, they began to make peace. They joined forces to conquer territories overseas and build up a vast empire. In 1921 southern Ireland left the Union to become a republic. Britain's political power declined in the 1900s, although it played a leading role in the two World Wars. By the 1960s the British Empire had broken up and most of Britain's colonies had become independent. In 1973 it joined the European Union.

Lloyds Building

The headquarters of Lloyds Bank was completed in 1986. It stands in the City of London, the financial centre of the UK.

Stonehenge

Some of the stones used to build the prehistoric temple at Stonehenge were dragged from a site 400 km away. It must have taken many years to build.

Carrauntoohill
1041m

Bant

N

Orkney Is.
Kirkwall
Thurso

Lerwick
Shetland Is.

Stornoway
Outer Hebrides

Skye
Loch Ness
Inverness
Peterhead

SCOTLAND
Aberdeen

Mallaig
▲Ben Nevis 1343m
Grampian Highlands
Tay

Oban
Perth
Dundee

ATLANTIC OCEAN

Glasgow
■ Edinburgh
Clyde

Ayr
Tweed
Southern Uplands

Londonderry
Newcastle
Tyne
Durham

NORTHERN IRELAND
Belfast
Stranraer
Carlisle
Middlesbrough

Sligo
Armagh
Lake District
Pennines
Swale

RELAND
Dundalk
Isle of Man
Blackpool
Leeds
Kingston-upon-Hull

Irish Sea

way
Athlone
Liffey
■ DUBLIN
Liverpool
Bradford
Manchester
Sheffield

Carlow
Wrexham
ENGLAND

erick
Tipperary
Derby
Nottingham

Cambrian Mts
Wolverhampton
Trent
Peterborough
Norwich

Waterford
Aberystwyth
Birmingham
Coventry
Cambridge

k
WALES
Wye
Severn
Northampton
Ipswich

Carmarthen
Luton
Colchester

Swansea
Gloucester
Oxford
■ LONDON
Canterbury

Cardiff ■
Bristol
Reading
Thames
Dover

ATLANTIC OCEAN
Exmoor
Salisbury
Southampton
Portsmouth
Folkestone
Brighton

Dartmoor
Exeter
Bournemouth

Land's End
Plymouth
English Channel

Penzance

CHANNEL ISLANDS

0 50 100 150 200 Kilometres
0   50   100 Miles

65

Industry

The UK is a major industrial nation. During the 1800s industries such as textiles, steel-making, shipbuilding and engineering were developed. They were fuelled by coal, the UK's biggest natural resource at that time. Recently, newer industries such as electronics, food processing and chemicals have grown in importance. Most people now work in services such as education, healthcare and tourism. Today the UK's most important natural resource is the large fields of oil and natural gas that lie beneath the North Sea.

In the Republic of Ireland, three out of five people live in towns or cities. Many have jobs in service industries or the manufacture of textiles and glass.

Irish fishermen

Two Irish fishermen pull a lobster pot back into shape before going to sea once again. Shellfish accounts for nearly a third of the Republic of Ireland's earnings from fishing. Ireland also has many lakes (loughs) and rivers teeming with trout and salmon.

■ **UNITED KINGDOM**
Population: 57,826,000
Currency: Pound sterling
Main exports: Manufactured goods

■ **ENGLAND**
Area: 130,420 sq km
Capital: London (6,680,000)
Official language: English

■ **WALES**
Area: 20,770 sq km
Capital: Cardiff (279,000)
Official languages: Welsh, English

■ **SCOTLAND**
Area: 77,170 sq km
Capital: Edinburgh (438,000)
Official language: English

■ **NORTHERN IRELAND**
Area: 14,120 sq km
Capital: Belfast (284,000)
Official language: English

■ **REPUBLIC OF IRELAND**
Area: 70,280 sq km
Population: 3,563,000
Capital: Dublin (916,000)
Official languages: Irish, English
Currency: Euro, Punt
Main exports: Livestock, dairy products, whiskey, machinery, chemicals, manufactured goods

United Kingdom

N. Ireland (unofficial)

England

Wales

Scotland

Republic of Ireland

Farming

In the UK only about two per cent of the population is employed in farming. However, much of the country is intensively farmed to produce grain, fruit and vegetables. Dairy cattle graze on the green pastures of western England and sheep feed on the uplands of Scotland and Wales. Much of the UK's ancient forest and woodland has been destroyed over the years, but large conifer plantations provide timber for building and paper-making.

Farming is vital to the economy of the Republic of Ireland. Its exports include butter, cheese and other dairy products, natural fibres, whiskey and beer.

Giant's Causeway
. . . .

The Giant's Causeway is a spectacular rock formation that forms part of the rugged coast of County Antrim in Northern Ireland.

Firth of Forth Bridge
. . . .

The Forth Bridge, opened in 1890, has two arches either side of Inchgarvie Island. About 55,000 tonnes of steel were used to build the bridge.

Cliffs of Dover
. . . .

The white cliffs of Dover on the English Channel symbolize home to English people returning by sea from the Continent.

Conflict in N. Ireland

Northern Ireland suffers from a political and religious divide. From 1969 a war raged there between the Irish Republican Army (IRA), Catholics who want the whole of Ireland to be an independent republic, and Protestant Loyalists, who want to maintain ties with Britain. A fragile peace declared in 1994 was followed by further violence.

Germany

Germany lies at the heart of Europe. Surrounded by nine other countries, its natural boundaries are two stretches of coastline in the north, the river Rhine in the southwest and the Bavarian Alps in the southeast. It is a fertile land with wide rivers and thick forests. Tourists visit all year round to enjoy beautiful scenery and fine architecture. Germany has rich natural resources, which have helped it rise above the devastation of the two World Wars to become one of the world's leading industrial nations. Its major cities are international centres of trade and banking.

Very few Germans work on the land. Most live in towns and cities, where the country's thriving industries are based. Since the 1950s many people from Turkey, Italy and Yugoslavia have also come to the country to work. Although this is a modern nation of urban-dwellers, old customs have not been forgotten. Some Germans still wear national dress

Fairs and festivals

A giant mask adds colour to the annual Museum Embankment festival held in Frankfurt. Carnivals are enjoyed throughout Germany.

for special occasions. Medieval traditions are preserved by townspeople who regularly perform plays that were written centuries ago.

Political protest has been common in western Germany since the 1960s. Today Germans often gather to protest about modern issues. These include pollution, nuclear power and the rise in racism that has recently occurred in Germany and other parts of Europe.

Ulm Cathedral

Ulm Cathedral was founded in 1377, but not completed until 1890. Its steeple is the tallest in the world, rising almost 161 m above the city on the river Danube.

68

N

DENMARK

NORTH SEA

BALTIC SEA

Flensburg

Kiel

Neumünster

Lübeck

Rostock

Stralsund

Schwerin

Wilhelmshaven

Bremerhaven

Hamburg

NETHERLANDS

Bremen

Lüneburg

Weser

Elbe

Oder

POLAND

Celle

Aller

BERLIN

Ems

Hannover

Brunswick

Brandenburg

Frankfurt an der Oder

Bielefeld

Weser

Hildesheim

Magdeburg

Harz Mts.

Leine

Münster

Paderborn

Elster

Dessau

Cottbus

Rhine

Essen

Dortmund

Kassel

Halle

Neisse

Duisburg

Wuppertal

Mühlhausen

Leipzig

Elbe

Düsseldorf

Aachen

Cologne

Bonn

Marburg

Erfurt

Dresden

Chemnitz

Geissen

Gera

Koblenz

Eifel

Wiesbaden

GERMANY

Zwickau

Plauen

Ore Mountains

Moselle

Rhine

Frankfurt-am-Main

Main

LUXEMBOURG

Trier

Mainz

Darmstadt

Würzburg

Bamberg

Bayreuth

CZECH REPUBLIC

Mannheim

Heidelberg

Nuremberg

FRANCE

Saarbrücken

Heilbronn

Bohemian Forest

Karlsruhe

Stuttgart

Danube

Ingolstadt

Regensburg

Passau

Rhine

Swabian Jura

Augsburg

Ulm

Munich

AUSTRIA

Freiburg

Black Forest

Lake Constance

ALPS

SWITZERLAND

▲ Zugspitze 2963m

0   50   100   150   Kilometres

0   25   50   75   100 Miles

69

Geography

Germany's low sandy coast looks out on to the stormy North Sea and Baltic Sea. The two seas are linked by the Kiel Canal, a busy shipping channel. Inland is a wide flat plain of heathland and timber plantations. Crops are grown in the broad river valleys. In the valley of the River Ruhr, rich deposits of coal and metal ores are mined.

In the centre is a rugged landscape of plateaus, forested mountains, gorges and rushing rivers. Vineyards and pasture where sheep graze cover the western hills, while wheat and barley grow in the fertile valleys. In the southwest lies the Black Forest, named for its dark fir trees. In the far southeast are the soaring Bavarian Alps. The highest point in Germany, the Zugspitze, is in this region.

Frankfurt stock exchange

Dealers are busy trading on the floor of the Frankfurt stock exchange. Frankfurt, on the river Main, is a major centre of industry and finance. The city often hosts international trade fairs.

History

People have lived here since ancient times. For most of its history this has been a divided land made up of many small states. Germany's defeat in World War I (1914-1918) left the country in crisis. The Nazis (National Socialists) came to power, promising to make Germany great again. Led by Adolf Hitler, the Nazis aimed to create a master race and killed millions of Jews, Poles, Russians and political opponents. Germany was defeated again in World War II (1939-1945) and separated into two parts – the Federal Republic of Germany in the west and the German Democratic Republic in the east. In 1990 the two parts were reunited amid great celebrations on both sides.

Wurst

Wurst means sausage and Germany is said to have over 1,500 different kinds! Wurst in rolls is often sold as a snack on the street.

■ **GERMANY**
Area: 356,730 sq km
Population: 81,187,000
Capital: Berlin (3,438,000)
Official language: German
Currency: Euro, Deutsche Mark
Main exports: Machinery, transport equipment, textiles, chemicals, iron, steel, minerals, wine, lignite

---

Economy

Germany is Europe's leading industrial nation. It is Europe's largest car manufacturer and a world leader in the production of chemicals for medicines, plastics and paints. In western Germany most farms are small and many are only operated part-time. In eastern Germany large farms that were run by the state are now being broken up and sold to individuals.

After World War II Germany's cities and factories were devastated and the country was divided. West Germany was helped by the USA, Britain and France to rebuild its economy. In 1957 it became a founder member of the European Union. East Germany was under communist rule and had state-run industries. It spent a lot of money on creating jobs and on social welfare, but had very few consumer goods. After reunification in 1990 the east joined the west's economic system, which caused high prices and unemployment in the east. These problems can be solved by Germany's strong economy.

The Bavarian Alps

Berchtesgaden is a ski resort set high up in the Bavarian Alps. Many mountaineers go there to climb Mount Watzmann.

Cologne Cathedral

The twin spires of the cathedral dominate Cologne's skyline. Building began in the 1200s but was not completed until 1880.

Switzerland, Austria and Liechtenstein

Switzerland is a land of towering snowy mountains, high waterfalls and long misty lakes. The Alps form a series of high ranges in the south and east, while the rainy conifer forests of the Jura Mountains line the western border with France. Below these peaks alpine pastures provide summer grazing for cattle and goats. Very little Swiss land is suitable for growing crops, except for hay and livestock fodder. Rushing rivers are dammed for hydro-electric power, but Switzerland has few other natural resources. Raw materials are imported and skilled craftspeople turn them into precision goods such as watches, clocks and electrical equipment.

About three-quarters of Austria lies in the snow-capped thickly forested Alps. Deer and small numbers of chamois live in these mountains. Austria has broad green valleys, rushing rivers and deep lakes. Cattle graze the high pastures while barley, rye

Hallstatt, Austria

This small market town rises steeply from the shore of Lake Halstatt. Because its cemetery suffers from lack of space, older bones are removed and stored on show in a charnel house in the mountainside.

and potatoes are grown in the Vienna Basin, the flat valley of the mighty river Danube. Much of the land is too rugged for agriculture, but by using modern farming methods Austria is able to produce three-quarters of the food its people need. Grapes are grown for wine. Timber for wood pulp and paper is cut from forests that are replanted according to strict conservation laws. Austria is a highly industrialized country, though most of its population now works in service industries such as retail, banking, tourism and healthcare.

Swiss fondue

Fondue is a dish of Swiss cheese heated in a pot with white wine. Bread is dipped into the cheese speared on forks. Fondue means melted in French.

Vienna's Burgtheater
• •

Vienna's imposing Burgtheater was built
in the late 1800s. At this time the capital
of Austria was one of the most important
cultural centres in the world. It was
particularly known for its rich musical life.

White-tailed eagle
• • • • • • • • • • • •

The survival of the white-tailed eagle is
now endangered. These majestic birds
have been hunted close to extinction. Some
may still be seen circling over the Austrian
Alps in winter.

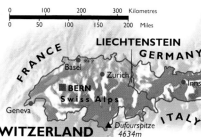

0   100   200   300   Kilometres
0   50   100   150   200   Miles

CZECH REPUBLIC

LIECHTENSTEIN
GERMANY

FRANCE

Basel

Zurich

• Linz

Donube

• Salzburg

VIENNA

• Innsbruck

AUSTRIA

■ BERN

Swiss Alps

▲ Grossglockner
3797m

Central Alps

Graz

HUNGARY

Geneva

I T A L Y

SWITZERLAND

▲ Dufourspitze
4634m

SLOVENIA

Liechtenstein

Liechtenstein was formed in 1719
when Prince Johann-Adam
Liechtenstein joined together the
two territories of Vaduz and
Schellenberg, formerly parts of
the Holy Roman Empire. His
descendants still rule here, though
laws are now passed by an elected
parliament. Women in
Liechtenstein did not gain the
right to vote until 1984.

N

Vaduz Castle, Liechtenstein
• •

*Vaduz Castle is the home of the Prince of
Liechtenstein. It overlooks a steep hillside
high above the country's capital. The
castle's fortifications date from the 1500s.*

Area: 41,130 sq km
Population: 6,938,000
Capital: Bern (299,000)
Official languages: German, French, Italian, Romansch
Currency: Swiss franc
Main exports: Machinery, chemicals, clocks and watches, precision instruments, textiles, clothes, foods including chocolate

■ AUSTRIA
Area: 83,860 sq km
Population: 7,988,000
Capital: Vienna (1,540,000)
Official language: German
Currency: Euro, Schilling
Main exports: Machinery, transport equipment, timber, paper and paper pulp, iron, steel, textiles

■ LIECHTENSTEIN
Area: 160 sq km
Population: 28,000
Capital: Vaduz (5,000)
Official language: German
Currency: Swiss franc
Main exports: Machinery, chemical products, textiles, pottery, dental products, stamps

Austria – history

The early inhabitants of Austria mined and traded in iron and salt. Celtic peoples moved here around 400BC, then in 15BC Austria was conquered by the Romans. From the 1200s a powerful family called the Habsburgs ruled Austria, making it the centre of a vast empire that grew to include Spain, Hungary and the Netherlands. Austria began to lose power in the 1800s and by 1918 the Habsburg empire was finished. The country was torn apart during the two World Wars, but since the 1950s Austria has built up its economy and become politically stable. It joined the European Union in 1995.

Tirol, Austria
. . . .

Hikers admire the view near Vent in the Tirol, the mountainous west of Austria. Walking and skiing are two favourite pastimes among the Austrian people.

● ● ● ● ● ● ● ● ● ● ● ● ● ● ● ● ● ● ● ●

Imaginatively dressed professional clowns perform stunts and mime in the streets of Vienna during Vienna festival week.

The Matterhorn, Switzerland
● ●

Chamois leap gracefully across the rocks beneath the east face of the Matterhorn, which stands on the Swiss-Italian border.

Switzerland – history

More than 2,000 years ago the Romans conquered the land that is now Switzerland, and called it the province of Helvetia. In 1921 the Swiss cantons, or provinces, began to fight to break away from the Holy Roman Empire. They gained independence in 1648.

Since 1815 the country has remained neutral, avoiding wars that have swept across Europe. Switzerland's neutrality has attracted many organizations that depend on international cooperation, such as the United Nations. Peace and stability have also helped the country prosper as a world centre of banking.

Liechtenstein – economy

Liechtenstein's population is no bigger than that of a small town. This country has strong ties with neighbouring Switzerland and uses Swiss currency. Dairy cattle graze the alpine pastures, while barley and fruit are grown in the valleys. However, only three per cent of the population works in agriculture. Since the 1950s Liechtenstein has become an industrialized nation with one of the highest standards of living in the world. Banking and tourism are its main industries, and the production of textiles, chemicals and pottery are also important. More revenue comes from the foreign businesses that have their headquarters here, attracted by Liechtenstein's low taxes.

75

France

France is a country of varied and beautiful landscapes, modern industries, historic towns and great cities. It has produced great thinkers, politicians, writers, painters, musicians, architects, scientists, film-makers and fashion designers. It is also famous for its wines and food, which are often said to be the best in the world. Each of France's 22 regions has its own traditional customs, foods and drinks, and several also have their own languages, although French is spoken everywhere.

The French Revolution of 1789 made France one of the first European nations to overthrow its king and set up a republic. The monarchy was restored for a time in the 1800s, but a republic was established once more in 1871. Since then, France has been a democratic republic almost continuously. The government is headed by a president, who appoints a prime minister. The capital, Paris, has long been the centre of power. However, the regions of France now have a greater say in government.

Sacré Coeur

Sacré Coeur Cathedral at the heart of Paris has long been a destination for pilgrims.

The majority of French people live in towns and cities. They work in manufacturing or service industries, such as education and catering. Their standard of living is high and most workers enjoy long summer holidays. In rural areas the majority work in agriculture and the countryside is dotted with small family farms and vineyards that are passed from one generation to the next.

Breton lacemaker

This woman is working a traditional lace mat. She is from Brittany, in northwest France. Her traditional dress includes a tall headdress made of lace called a coiffe.

N

CORSICA
(France)

Bastia

Ajaccio

Bonifacio

0 50 100 150 200 Kilometres
0   50   100 Miles

Dunkerque
Calais
Boulogne
Lille
Arras

BELGIUM

LUXEMBOURG

GERMANY

English Channel

Cherbourg
Le Havre
Caen
Rouen
Dieppe
Amiens
Charleville-Mézières

St.-Malo
Reims
Metz
Marne
Strasbourg
Nancy
Moselle
Vosges Mountains
Colmar
Mulhouse
Rhine

PARIS
Chartres
Châlons-sur-Marne

FRANCE

Fontainebleau
Seine
Troyes

Rennes
Le Mans
Orléans
Loire

Angers
Tours
Loire
Cher
Bourges

Nantes

Dijon
Besançon
Saône
Doubs

Jura Mountains

SWITZERLAND

Poitiers

La Rochelle
Montluçon
Mâcon
Saône

Limoges
Clermont-Ferrand
Lyon
Rhône

Cognac
Mt. Dore 1886m
St-Etienne
Isère
Mt. Blanc 4807m

Central Massif
Isère
Grenoble

Bordeaux
Dordogne
Cère
Valence
Drac
Alps

ITALY

of cay
Lot
Lot
Rhône
Durance

Garonne
Aveyron
Avignon
Durance
Verdon
MONACO

Montauban
Tarn
Nîmes
Aix-en-Provence
Nice

ritz
Adour
Toulouse
Montpellier
Cannes

Bayonne
Garonne
Carcassonne
Béziers
Marseille

Pau
Ariège
Aude
Toulon

Lourdes
Pyrenees
Perpignan
Mediterranean Sea

SPAIN
ANDORRA

■ **FRANCE**
Area: 543,970 sq km
Population: 57,660,000
Capital: Paris (9,319,000)
Official language: French
Currency: Euro, French franc
Main exports: Wine, agricultural products, machinery, transport equipment, chemicals

■ **MONACO**
Area: 1.9 sq km
Population: 28,000
Capital: Monaco (1,500)
Official language: French
Currency: French franc
Main exports: Chemicals, pharmaceuticals, precision instruments

France

Monaco

Pont du Gard
• • • • • • • • • • •

This Roman aqueduct was built to carry fresh water to the city of Nimes in southern France. The Romans built many fine cities and roads during their occupation of France from about 50BC until the AD400s.

Economy

Rich farmland and a mild climate make France an important agricultural nation. Wheat, sugar beet, vegetables and apples are grown in the north. Dairy cattle graze the lush pastures of the northwest, producing creamy butters and cheeses. Vines growing grapes for the wine industry flourish all over the country. In the south and southwest there are fields of sunflowers and maize, as well as orchards of peaches, plums and cherries. A large timber industry is based on the country's vast forests.

France's natural resources include bauxite (used to make aluminium), iron ore, coal and oil. Mountain streams and rivers are harnessed to produce hydro-electric power and France has also built many nuclear power stations. French factories produce chemicals, textiles, and electronic equipment. About half the labour force works in service industries.

Monaco
• •

The tiny principality of Monaco attracts visitors from all over the world who come to gamble in its famous casinos and gaming halls.

A varied landscape

The French climate is mild and rainy along the Atlantic coast, but further inland, the summers are hot and the winters cold. The landscape is immensely varied. In the north are fertile plains crossed by broad meandering rivers. To the west, craggy headlands jut into the stormy Atlantic. In the east, forested hills rise to high snow-capped mountains, and in the south, sunny beaches line the glittering Mediterranean Sea. France's borders are marked by mountains. The Vosges and Jura ranges run along the German and Swiss frontiers, and the Pyrenees join France to Spain. The mighty Alps rise along the Italian border, with gleaming glaciers and walls of rock towering above mountain pastures where cattle graze.

Provence
• • • • • • • • • • • • • • •

Fields of scented lavender colour a hillside in Provence, south of France. Lavender and other flowers including roses are used to make perfume at Grasse, the international centre of the industry.

Quiche Lorraine
• • • • • • • • • •

This dish comes from Lorraine, in northeastern France. The crisp pastry shell is filled with beaten eggs, cream, cheese, seasoning and chopped bacon.

Pyrenean desman
• • • • • • • • • • • • • • • • • • •

The Pyrenean desman, a long-nosed water mole, lives in the fast-flowing streams of the Pyrenees. Pollution is threatening its survival.

Spain and Portugal

Spain and Portugal are cut off from the rest of Europe by the rocky Pyrenees, a range of snow-capped mountains. The two countries together form the Iberian Peninsula. Spain's interior is a plateau, a vast area of high flat ground that is hot and dusty in summer. High rainfall to the north makes the coast there green and fertile. In the south, a fierce sun beats down on vineyards and groves of olives and oranges. Because most of Spain has such little rain, farmers need to irrigate their crops by pumping water to them.

Many Spaniards are employed in industry, and Spain is one of the largest car manufacturers in Europe. Others work in catering and tourism, looking after the visitors who come to enjoy their country's warm climate and golden beaches.

Portugal lies to the west of Spain, on the Atlantic Ocean. The north of the country is rocky, with a mild, damp climate, while the south is flat, and very hot in summer. Much of the land is covered in forests of valuable cork oaks. Cork from these trees is exported all over the world, and so is port, one of the wines for which Portugal is famous.

80

N

Bay of Biscay

Santander
San Sebastián
FRANCE
Bilbao
Vitoria
Pamplona
Pyrenees
ANDORRA
Andorra la Vella
Burgos
Logroño
Ebro
Arga
Gállego
Cinca
Llobregat
Figueras
Gerona
Soria
Duero
Ebro
Jalón
Saragossa
Lérida
Manresa
Tarrasa
Barcelona
SPAIN
Caspe
Reus
Tarragona
Tajuna
Tortosa
Guadalajara
Tajo
Tajo
Alcalá de Henares
Teruel
Morella
Vinaroz
MADRID
Mijares
Aranjuez
Cuenca
Castellón de la Plana
Toledo
Turia
MENORCA
MALLORCA
Mahón
Palma
Manacor
Villarrobledo
Júcar
Albacete
Valencia
IBIZA
Ciudad Real
Alcoy
Ibiza
Puertollano
Segura
Alicante
Mediterranean Sea
Linares
Murcia
Jaén
Lorca
Cartagena
Granada
Aguilas
Sierra
Nevada
Almería
Motril

The Parade of the Giants

• •

*The Parade of the Giants takes place every
year in Toledo. Children and grown-ups dress
up in masks as devils, animals and clowns
and sing and dance through the streets.*

81

People

The people of the Iberian peninsula are very diverse. The Basque people of the north speak Euskara, a language not connected with any other in Europe. The Galicians of the far northwest trace their history back to the ancient Celts, and their traditions include bagpipe-playing. In the south, the influence of Moorish conquerors can still be seen in the architecture and farming methods, while Romany gypsies have left their mark on the passionate singing and dancing of flamenco. Everyone joins together to celebrate the many religious festivals, fairs and fiestas. Most people enjoy watching bullfights. Because of the fierce heat, businesses close in the middle of the day and people take a siesta (sleep) after lunch.

History

About 5,000 years ago the Iberians came to Spain and Portugal from North Africa. Later on, Greeks, Romans and Moors from North Africa also settled. In the 1400s explorers from Spain and Portugal conquered much of South America. They also established colonies in Africa and Asia. From the 1600s their power declined as their colonies broke away. During the 1900s, Spain and Portugal were ruled by harsh dictators. In the 1970s they became democracies. Today both belong to the European Union.

■ **SPAIN**
Area: 504,750 sq km
Population: 39,143,000
Capital: Madrid (2,910,000)
Official language: Spanish
Currency: Euro, Peseta
Main exports: Vehicles, wine, machinery, fruit, vegetables, olive oil, chemicals, textiles, iron, steel

■ **ANDORRA**
Area: 450 sq km
Population: 48,000
Capital: Andorra la Vella (19,000)
Official language: Catalan
Currency: French franc, Spanish peseta
Main exports: Clothes, mineral water, tobacco

■ **PORTUGAL**
Area: 91,830 sq km
Population: 9,860,000
Capital: Lisbon (831,000)
Official language: Portuguese
Currency: Euro, Escudo
Main exports: Clothes, textiles, cork, port and other wines, machinery, transport equipment, footwear, paper, timber products, canned fish

Portugal

Andorra

The Monument to the Discoveries

. . . .

This sculpture in Portugal's capital Lisbon was erected in the 1960s. It celebrates the Portuguese explorers of the 1400s.

La Mezquita, Cordoba, Spain

During the early AD700s Spain was conquered by the Moors from North Africa. The spectacular mosque in Cordoba with its colonnades and striped archways dates from that time.

Portuguese cooper

A cooper (barrel-maker) cuts staves for the big wooden barrels used to store port, a sweet after-dinner wine.

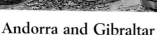

Velez-Blanco

The castle of Velez-Blanco crowns a rugged hilltop in Andalucia, southern Spain. It was built in the 1500s by Italians.

Andorra and Gibraltar

Most people in the tiny mountainous country of Andorra live in the valley of the Valira River. They process tobacco, graze sheep or grow potatoes. Others work in the tourist trade. Andorra also makes money by selling cheap goods in low-tax stores, and by the sale of stamps. Native Andorrans are descended from a people called Catalans, who have their own language. Most non-Catalans speak Spanish.

Gibraltar is no more than a limestone rock, but it has strategic importance because it juts out towards Africa at the neck of the Mediterranean Sea. Britain seized Gibraltar from Spain in the 1700s and it remains a British colony and naval base. The land frontier between Gibraltar and Spain was reopened in 1983. Most people on Gibraltar work at the naval base or in the tourist industry.

Strange rock formations

A pillar of eroded rock shimmers in the summer heat on the edge of the Meseta, Spain's central plateau.

Italy and its neighbours

AUSTRIA

SWITZERLAND

A   L   P   S

Bolzano
▲ Mt. Ortles
3905m

Udine

SLOVENIA

▲ Mt. Blanc
4807m

Bergamo

Brescia

Verona

Trieste

Ticino

Milan

Piave

Venice

FRANCE

Turin

Tanaro

Oglio

Padua

Po

▲ Mt. Viso
3841m

Parma

Modena

Ferrara

Reno

Bologna

Ravenna

CROATIA

Genoa

La Spezia

Rimini

San Marino

MONACO

Pisa

Arno

Florence

SAN MARINO

Ancona

Adriatic Sea

Ligurian Sea

Livorno

A   p   e   n   n   i   n   e   s

Perugia

Bastia

Elba

Terni

Pescara

**CORSICA
(France)**

Tiber

Ajaccio

ROME

ITALY

Foggia

**VATICAN
CITY**

Ofanto

Bonifacio

Naples

Potenza

Mt. Vesuvius ▲
1277m

Salerno

Tar

Sassari

Seni

Tirso

Tyrrhenian Sea

Oristano

Cosenza

**SARDINIA
(Italy)**

Cagliari

| 0 | 50 | 100 | 150 | 200 | 250 | Kilometres |
| 0 | 50 | | 100 | | 150 | Miles |

**Lipari
Islands**

Cata

Palermo

Messina

Reggio di
Calabria

N

Trapani

▲ Mt. Etna
3340m

**SICILY
(Italy)**

Catania

Agrigento

Syracuse

Mediterranean Sea

MALTA

■ Valletta

84

Italy is a peninsula that sticks into the Mediterranean Sea like a boot. The country also includes Sicily, Sardinia and a number of smaller islands. Vatican City State and San Marino are two tiny independent countries within the Italian mainland. The Republic of Malta, a British colony from 1814 to 1964, consists of two Mediterranean islands, Malta and Gozo.

Italy enjoys mild, damp winters, but its hills and mountains can be cold and snowy. The summers are warm, with the southern and coastal plains becoming extremely hot and dusty. Regional differences in Italy are very strong, in everything from food to local customs. The way of life in wealthy northern cities such as Milan, Turin,

Venice

• •

A vaporetto (water bus) chugs past the church of Santa Maria della Salute on Venice's Grand Canal. Venice is a city of canals where everyone travels by boat.

Bologna and Genoa is also very different from that of poor farming communities of the south.

Most Italians live in towns or cities, working mainly in service and manufacturing industries. Only nine per cent still work in agriculture and in rural areas many farmhouses have been turned into holiday homes.

Sardinia

• •

Masked riders take part in a horse race called the sartiglia *during the annual carnival in Oristano, on Sardinia's west coast.*

rindisi

History

Two thousand years ago this land was the heart of the Roman empire. It ruled much of Western Europe as well as territories all round the Mediterranean Sea. The Romans' language, Latin, is at the root of several modern European languages, including Italian and French. The influence of Roman architecture, laws, literature and road-building is still felt right across Europe today.

The Roman empire collapsed in AD476. The Italian peninsula split into a collection of cities and small states, although the city of Rome remained powerful as the centre of the Roman Catholic Church. In the Middle Ages many of the independent cities grew wealthy through trade and banking. They became centres of art and science during the Renaissance, a time when new ideas swept through Europe.

From the 1500s some parts of Italy were ruled by France, Spain and Austria. Others were controlled by the Pope. Italy finally threw off foreign rule and united as an independent kingdom in 1861. In 1922 a fascist dictator, Benito Mussolini, came to power. He led Italy into World War II. Since 1947 Italy has been a democratic republic and a major industrial country.

The Leaning Tower of Pisa
• •

Pisa's leaning bell tower (1360s) was built of marble on sinking ground. Engineering work stops it from collapsing.

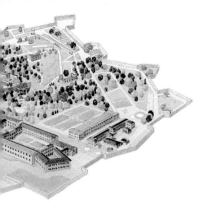

Vatican City

Vatican City, the world's smallest country, lies within the city of Rome. It is the headquarters of the Catholic Church, headed by the Pope. Its main buildings are St Peter's Basilica and the Papal Palace.

Economy

Italy is the world's leading wine-maker. It is also a major producer of olives and olive oil. Northern Italy has become one of the richest and most advanced industrial areas of Europe, hosting major international trade fairs as well as manufacturing cars, chemicals and textiles. Milan is a famous fashion centre and Italian clothes, shoes and leather goods are exported all over the world.

Goods for export overseas pass through the major ports of Genoa and Trieste. Italy has a large fleet of merchant ships as well as many fishing fleets, which catch tuna and sardines in the Mediterranean Sea. Over half of Italy's trade is with member states of the European Union. However, service industries such as tourism now generate more income than manufacturing.

■ ITALY
Area: 301,300 sq km
Population: 57,057,000
Capital: Rome (2,724,000)
Official language: Italian
Currency: Euro, Italian lira
Main exports: Wine, machinery, transport equipment, footwear, clothes, olive oil, textiles, mineral products

■ SAN MARINO
Area: 61 sq km
Population: 23,000
Capital: San Marino (4,500)
Official language: Italian
Currency: Italian lira
Main exports: Wine, machinery, chemicals

■ VATICAN CITY
Area: 0.4 sq km
Population: about 1,000

■ MALTA
Area: 310 sq km
Population: 361,000
Capital: Valletta (102,000)
Official languages: Maltese, English
Currency: Maltese lira
Main exports: Machinery, clothes, textiles, transport equipment, ships, beverages, tobacco

Maltese harbour

A fisherman mends his nets in Malta's Marsa harbour. The picturesque town is a popular destination for tourists.

Poland and its neighbours

Baltic Sea

0 50 100 150 200 250 300 Kilometres
0 50 100 150 Miles

KALININGRAD (Russia)

LITHUANIA

N

Gdansk

Szczecin

Bydgoszez

BELARUS

Poznan

Oder

Vistula

Bug

WARSAW

POLAND

Lodz

GERMANY

Neisse

Sudetes Mts.

Wroclaw

Lublin

Ore Mts.

Elbe

Oder

Katowice

UKRAINE

PRAGUE

Ostrava

Krakow

Plzen

CZECH REPUBLIC

Carpathian Mountains

Brno

▲ Rysy 2499m

SLOVAK REPUBLIC

Kosice

AUSTRIA

BRATISLAVA

Miskolc

Danube

Debrecen

BUDAPEST

ROMANIA

Lake Balaton

HUNGARY

SLOVENIA

Pecs

Danube

Szeged

CROATIA

YUGOSLAVIA

Slovak musician

A Slovak musician plays a zither. The strings are plucked with a plectrum, a pick attached to a ring on the musician's thumb.

Much of Poland is covered by the vast open plains and rolling hills that stretch eastwards from Germany and on into Russia. Potatoes and rye are grown in the plains of central Poland. The most fertile land, on the hills of the south, produces wheat and maize. Cattle and sheep graze the southern pastures. In the far south of the country are forested mountains, which are home to bears and wolves. The Baltic coastal region to the north has thousands of lakes connected by rivers and streams and is dotted with peat bogs. Many Poles spend their leisure time in this area, windsurfing, fishing, yachting and canoeing.

The Poles are a Slavic people who founded a powerful state in central Europe in the AD800s. From the 1300s to the 1600s this state became the centre of a great empire. The empire declined and was divided between Russia, Prussia and Austria in 1795. Independence was won back in 1918, but during World War II Poland was overrun by the Soviet Union and Nazi Germany.

Cesky Krumlov

The town of Cesky Krumlov stands amid wooded hills in the Czech Republic. It was founded in the 1200s and many of its buildings date from the Middle Ages. It became wealthy through silver mining.

Towards democracy

Nazi rule was brutal and millions of Poles were murdered. From 1947 Poland was governed by communists. During the 1970s and 1980s workers protested against bad living conditions with strikes and riots, demanding better pay and political reform. In 1989 democratic elections were won by Solidarity, the popular workers' party. The changeover from communism to democracy increased people's freedom, but at first it also brought widespread unemployment and high prices.

Up until the 1940s Poland's economy was based mainly on agriculture and most people lived and worked in rural areas. Today the majority live in cities. They work in service industries such as healthcare, education and finance, or in heavy industries producing coal, steel and machinery.

Polish floral statues

These floral statues represent figures from Polish folklore. During the communist era Polish traditions were suppressed. Today Poles are free to celebrate their national identity.

89

Hungary

Hungary's farmland is its chief resource. Crops of maize, wheat, potatoes and sugar beet thrive in its rich black soil. Grapes and other fruit are grown for making wine and jams for export. Most farms are family collectives.

Communists took over the Hungarian government in 1948 and began a programme of intensive industrialization. They restricted personal freedom and controlled wages and prices. When the Hungarians revolted in 1956, tanks rolled in from the communist Soviet Union to support the government and crush the rebellion. Many were killed or imprisoned. The government relaxed restrictions and democratic elections were held in 1990. Today most people live in cities and work in factories or service industries. The government is working to clean up industrial pollution left by the communist era.

Czech Republic

The Czech Republic is a country of fertile plains, wooded hills and rugged mountains.

In 1918 the Czechs joined with their neighbours, the Slovaks, to form a new country called Czechoslovakia. From 1948 it was governed by communists, supported by the Soviet Union. The Czechoslovak communists demanded political reform in 1968, but their protest was squashed by Soviet troops.

Goulash
. . . .

Goulash is Hungary's national dish. It is a rich stew made with meat and potatoes and flavoured with paprika and soured cream. Goulash is served with noodles and black bread.

Poland's capital
. . . .

Poland's capital, Warsaw, is a centre of finance and administration. Heavy industries were set up here during the communist era when all factories were owned by the state. Today they are returning to private ownership.

Prague, Czech Republic
•••••••••••••••••••••••

A series of bridges spans the broad Vltava River in the beautiful, old city of Prague, the capital of the Czech Republic. Prague has been a rich commercial centre since the Middle Ages.

Then in 1989 a general strike triggered democratic elections. In 1993 Czechoslovakia was peacefully divided into two new independent countries – the Czech Republic and Slovakia. The Czech Republic includes former Czechoslovakia's industrial areas. Its factories produce steel, glass, machinery, paper and beer.

Slovakia

Slovakia is a land of mountains, lakes and forests. The country was created in 1993 when Czechoslovakia split into two separate states. At first Slovakia faced economic problems because it had little manufacturing industry. Slovakia's natural resources are timber, iron ore and the rich farmland around the river Danube, where farmers grow cereal crops and rear pigs. Around 40 per cent of Slovaks work in industry, many producing consumer goods.

■ **POLAND**
Area: 312,680 sq km
Population: 38,459,000
Capital: Warsaw (1,655,000)
Official language: Polish
Currency: Zloty
Main exports: Copper, coal, machinery, vehicles, footwear

■ **SLOVAKIA**
Area: 49,040 sq km
Population: 5,318,000
Capital: Bratislava (441,000)
Official language: Slovak
Currency: Koruna
Main exports: Iron ore, chemicals, petroleum products, steel, weapons

■ **CZECH REPUBLIC**
Area: 78,860 sq km
Population: 10,328,000
Capital: Prague (1,215,000)
Official language: Czech
Currency: Koruna
Main exports: Machinery, transport equipment, chemicals, iron, steel

■ **HUNGARY**
Area: 93,030 sq km
Population: 10,294,000
Capital: Budapest (2,000,000)
Official language: Hungarian
Currency: Forint
Main exports: Consumer goods, raw materials, agricultural products, machinery, transport equipment

---

Poland

Hungary

Czech Republic

Slovakia

The Balkans and Romania

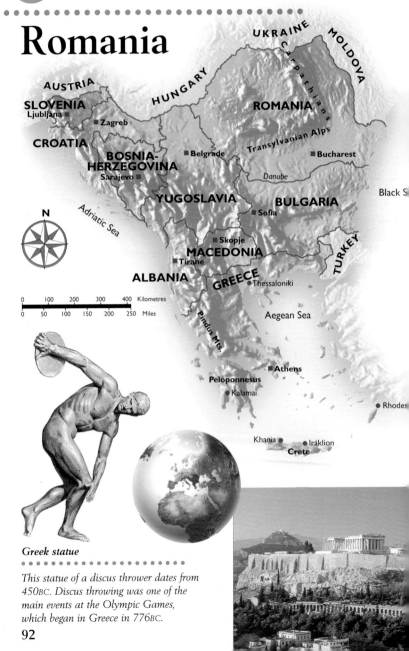

AUSTRIA

SLOVENIA
Ljubljana

■ Zagreb

CROATIA

BOSNIA-
HERZEGOVINA
Sarajevo ■

HUNGARY

UKRAINE

Carpathians

MOLDOVA

ROMANIA

Transylvanian Alps

■ Belgrade

■ Bucharest

Danube

YUGOSLAVIA

BULGARIA

■ Sofia

Black S

■ Skopje

MACEDONIA
■ Tirane

ALBANIA

GREECE ● Thessaloniki

TURKEY

Adriatic Sea

Aegean Sea

Pindus Mts.

■ Athens

Peloponnesus

● Kalamai

● Rhodes

Khania ● ● Iráklion

Crete

N

| 0 | 100 | 200 | 300 | 400 | Kilometres |
| 0 | 50 | 100 | 150 | 200 | 250 Miles |

Greek statue

*This statue of a discus thrower dates from
450BC. Discus throwing was one of the
main events at the Olympic Games,
which began in Greece in 776BC.*

This area takes its name from the Balkan Mountains of Bulgaria. In these eight countries craggy mountains that are difficult to cross separate various groups of people with different languages, customs and religions. Over the centuries these isolated communities have often fought for each other's territory.

The spectacularly rugged Adriatic coast is fringed with mountainous islands. Crops such as maize, fruit and tobacco are grown along the coast and in the fertile plains of the Danube Basin. Tourism is an important source of income across the whole area. In the former Yugoslavia huge efforts are being made to restore historic towns and cities and to rebuild homes and factories devastated by war.

Macedonian church

The church of St John at Caneo overlooks beautiful Lake Ohrid. Christianity is the main religion in Macedonia, but there are also many Muslims here.

A land of many islands

Greece occupies the southern part of the Balkan Peninsula. It includes hundreds of beautiful islands scattered in the deep blue Aegean and Ionian seas. The largest island is Crete, which lies farther south in the Mediterranean Sea. Greece has natural harbours, mountains and deep valleys. It is a rocky land of limestone covered in scrub and scented wild herbs grazed by flocks of sheep and goats. The earth is carpeted with flowers in spring but baked brown and dusty during the hot summer months. Olive groves and wheatfields surround peaceful whitewashed villages. However, Greece's cities, with their mix of ancient and modern buildings, are busy with people and traffic. Air pollution from cars and factories in Athens is threatening health and eating away at the many national monuments.

Greek salad

Greek salad is made with tomatoes, onions, chillies, cucumber, black olives and cubes of feta cheese. It is sprinkled with herbs and olive oil. Crusty bread and a Greek wine called retsina often accompany this dish.

Acropolis, Greece

The Acropolis is a rocky fortress on a hill above Athens. The Parthenon, on its highest point, is a temple built in 438BC.

History

The first great European civilization began in Greece in about 2500BC. The ancient Greeks developed the idea of democracy, or rule by the people. Since the fall of the Greek empire, these lands have come under the rule of the Roman empire, Austria-Hungary and the Ottoman empire. After World War II much of the area fell under communist rule.

Communism collapsed in 1990 and Yugoslavia, which was a union of six republics including Croatia, Bosnia and Serbia, broke up into separate nations. When Croatia and Bosnia declared independence in 1991 and 1992 the Serbs living in those countries objected and began a brutal civil war. Thousands were killed or forced to flee their homes. Peace talks led to the Dayton Accord of 1995. Under this agreement, Bosnia-Herzegovina now consists of a Croat-Muslim province and a Serb province.

Economy

Under communist rule, which affected all these countries

Roman amphitheatre

• •

The huge amphitheatre at Pula in Croatia was built by the Romans in AD80. People came here to watch gladiators and wild animals fighting to the death.

except Greece, businesses and farms were taken into state ownership. The communists built many factories, but most people lived in rural areas where poverty was common. Today two-thirds of the people live in cities. Many work in industry or tourism. The seafaring nation of Greece has important shipping and fishing industries. Rich deposits of iron, oil and natural gas have brought new wealth to Albania.

Dalmatian pelican

• • • • • • • • • • • •

Dalmatian pelicans can be seen fishing in the delta of the river Danube on the Black Sea coast. Drainage of wetland and hunting have reduced their numbers.

Albanian apples

• •

Women sort apples at a factory at Peshkepi, in eastern Albania. Fresh fruit, canned fruit, jams and juices are important to the Albanian economy.

■ ROMANIA
Area: 237,500 sq km
Population: 22,755,000
Capital: Bucharest (2,351,000)
Official language: Romanian
Currency: Leu
Main exports: Petroleum products, oilfield equipment, cement

■ GREECE
Area: 131,960 sq km
Population: 10,350,000
Capital: Athens (3,097,000)
Official language: Greek
Currency: Drachma
Main exports: Clothes, olive oil, petroleum products, fruit, tobacco

■ BULGARIA
Area: 110,990 sq km
Population: 8,469,000
Capital: Sofia (1,142,000)
Official language: Bulgarian
Currency: Lev
Main exports: Machinery, food, wine, tobacco, fuels and raw materials

■ ALBANIA
Area: 28,750 sq km
Population: 3,338,000
Capital: Tirane (251,000)
Official language: Albanian
Currency: Lek
Main exports: Iron ore, natural gas, oil, chrome, bitumen, nickel, copper

■ SLOVENIA
Area: 20,250 sq km
Population: 1,990,000
Capital: Ljubljana (268,000)
Official language: Slovenian
Currency: Tolar
Main exports: Machinery, transport equipment, raw materials, food

■ CROATIA
Area: 56,540 sq km
Population: 4,789,000
Capital: Zagreb (727,000)
Official language: Serbo-Croatian
Currency: Kuna
Main exports: Chemicals, clothes, food, machinery

■ BOSNIA-HERZEGOVINA
Area: 51,130 sq km
Population: 4,366,000
Capital: Sarajevo (526,000)
Official language: Serbo-Croatian
Currency: Dinar (a new currency, the Marka, is planned)
Main exports: Clothes, chemicals, furniture, machinery

■ MACEDONIA
Area: 25,710 sq km
Population: 2,173,000
Capital: Skopje (449,000)
Official language: Macedonian
Currency: Denar
Main exports: Chemicals, clothes, footwear, machinery, transport equipment, food, textiles

■ YUGOSLAVIA
Area: 102,170 sq km
Population: 10,485,000
Capital: Belgrade (1,169,000)
Official language: Serbo-Croatian
Currency: Dinar
Main exports: Textiles, chemicals, clothes, food, iron, steel, machinery, transport equipment, manufactured goods

Romania

Croatia

Greece

Slovenia

Macedonia

Bulgaria

Yugoslavia

Bosnia-Herzegovina

Albania

Russia and its neighbours

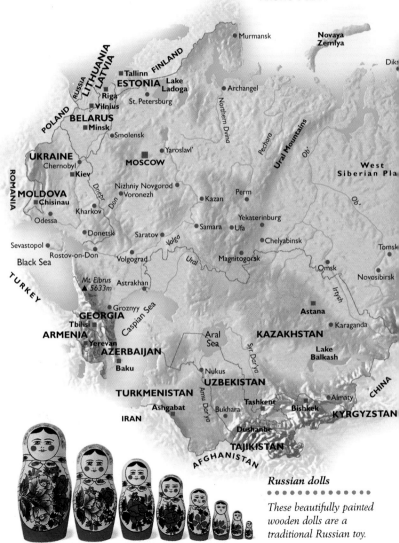

ARCTIC OCEAN

Murmansk

Novaya Zemlya

Diks

RUSSIA
LITHUANIA
LATVIA
FINLAND
POLAND
■ Tallinn
ESTONIA
Lake Ladoga
Riga ■
Vilnius ■
St. Petersburg
● Archangel

Northern Dvina
Pechora
Ural Mountains
Ob'

BELARUS
■ Minsk
● Smolensk
● Yaroslavl'

UKRAINE
Chernobyl
● Kiev
MOSCOW ■
Dnepr

ROMANIA
MOLDOVA
■ Chisinau
● Odessa

Nizhniy Novgorod ●
● Voronezh
Don
● Kazan
Perm ●
West Siberian Pla

Ob'

Kharkov
Saratov
Volga
Yekaterinburg
● Samara ● Ufa
Chelyabinsk ●
Tomsk ●

Sevastopol ●
Rostov-on-Don
Volgograd
Ural
Magnitogorsk ●
Omsk ●
Novosibirsk ●

Black Sea
TURKEY

Donetsk ●

Irtysh

Mt. Elbrus
▲ 5633m
Astrakhan
Groznyy
Caspian Sea

■ Astana
● Karaganda

GEORGIA
Tbilisi ■
ARMENIA
● Yerevan
AZERBAIJAN
● Baku

Aral Sea
Syr Darya
KAZAKHSTAN
Lake Balkash

Nukus ●
UZBEKISTAN
Amu Darya

TURKMENISTAN
● Ashgabat
IRAN
Bukhara ●
Tashkent ■
Almaty ●
Bishkek ■
CHINA
KYRGYZSTAN

Dushanbe ■
TAJIKISTAN
AFGHANISTAN

Russian dolls

These beautifully painted wooden dolls are a traditional Russian toy.

0 250 500 750 1000 Kilometres
0   250   500   750 Miles

N

Severnaya Zemlya

New Siberian Islands

Anadyr'

Bering Sea

Kolyma

Indigirka

Verkhoyansk Range

Lena

RUSSIA

East

Kamchatka Peninsula

Magadan

Central Siberian Plateau

Siberian

Nizhnyaya Tunguska

Yakutsk

Uplands

Sea of Okhotsk

Lena

Kuril Islands

Sakhalin

Angara

Amur

Krasnoyarsk

Irkutsk **Lake Baikal**

Khabarovsk

CHINA

Yenisey

Ulan-Ude

MONGOLIA

Vladivostok

JAPAN

Russian trawler

• • • • • • • • • • • • • • • • • • •

The catch taken by this Russian trawler is frozen on board ready for delivery to a fish processing factory. Fishing is an important part of the Russian economy. Both fresh and preserved fish are favourite foods with the Russian people.

Russia is the largest country in the world. It covers over 17 million square kilometres, borders 14 other countries and crosses eight time zones. Extending north to the frozen wastes that lie above the Arctic Circle, its expanses also take in vast forests, high mountains and wide plains. Russia has long bitter winters and short summers. Snow can cover more than half the country for six months a year, so it can be difficult to make the most of the many natural resources available. These resources include large regions of farmland and plentiful reserves of timber, oil, coal and natural gas. The bitter cold means that few people live in the north, part of an area called Siberia. Political prisoners used to be sent to Siberian labour camps.

Revolution

For centuries Russia was a vast empire ruled by emperors called tsars. The tsars kept working people living in poverty so the upper classes could live in luxury. From the 1600s to the 1800s the workers' discontent with the tsars erupted into revolts. By the early 1900s revolutionary groups had emerged and in 1917 a group called the Bolsheviks led a revolution under Lenin. Tsar Nicholas II was killed and Lenin set up a communist government, forming the Union of Soviet Socialist Republics (USSR).

Collapse of communism

Lenin's successor, Joseph Stalin, ruled by terror from 1929 until 1953. The 1940s to the 1980s marked a period of distrust between the West and communist countries in the East, which is often called the Cold War. When Mikhail Gorbachev became president in the 1980s he introduced reforms that gave the people greater freedom. At this time some republics began to demand independence. By the early 1990s communism had collapsed and most republics were independent.

Borscht
● ● ● ● ● ● ● ● ● ● ● ●

Borscht is a classic Russian soup and can be eaten hot or cold. It has beetroot as its main ingredient.

Cotton harvest
● ●

Cotton, harvested from the fields of Bokhara in Uzbekistan, is piled into fluffy heaps ready for sorting, processing, and weaving into fabric. Cotton is Uzbekistan's most important export.

Kalta Minar mosque, Uzbekistan
• • • • • • • • • • • • • • • • • • • •

This tiled minaret was intended to be the tallest in Central Asia, but building stopped when ruler Mohammed Khan died in 1855.

Grain harvest
• •

Combine harvesters work the fields on a government-owned Russian farm. Russia's vast areas of farmland make it one of the world's major grain producers.

Geography

Most of the area on the map lies in the Asian continent, but western Russia, Moldova, Belarus, Ukraine and the Baltic States lie in Europe. The Ural Mountains are usually considered to divide Europe and Asia.

The Russian climate includes great extremes, growing hotter towards the south and colder and drier towards the east and north. Tundra covers much of the most northerly region. Little grows on this frozen plain and few people live there. Below this region a belt of dense forest sprawls across the land. Taiga (coniferous forest) covers the northern part of the belt. The soil is mainly too poor to grow crops. Farther south the forest becomes mixed coniferous and deciduous trees. The climate here is milder and some areas can be farmed.

Rolling plains known as steppes start below the forests. The Caucasus Mountains and the Caspian Sea form Russia's southernmost area. The slopes of the Caucasus Mountains have lush, green, fertile meadows, while the Urals contain important deposits of iron and copper.

A Polish Roman Catholic church rises against the skyline in Minsk, the capital of Belarus. Very few old buildings remain in the city, which was badly damaged during World War II.

Towards capitalism

After communism collapsed government price controls were lifted. Under capitalism, producers could charge what they liked for goods, and prices soared. However, incomes remained very low and this caused severe economic problems. Shortages were just as common as they had been under communism, because ordinary people could not afford to pay for goods. Today economic hardship continues and shoppers jostle each other to buy food on the black (illegal) market. Heavy industry, farming and mining still form the backbone of the economy and new ways are being found to exploit mineral resources.

Communist economy

When communism ended with the break-up of the Soviet Union in 1991, the newly independent states had to make the huge and very difficult change in their economy from communism to capitalism. The word *soviet* means a council elected by the people and the basis of communism was that everybody should share both the work and the profits. Communist law stated that the government of the Soviet Union owned all the country's factories and farms as well as controlling wages and prices. Any profits were shared by the people and no one was allowed to run a private business. From the 1920s onwards the Soviet Union became a heavily industrialized nation. The government set up factories and mines all over the country. Huge state farms were created and farming practices were modernized with the use of pesticides and fertilizers to increase yields.

100

The Russian people

The majority of Russians are descended from a people called Slavs, but there are small numbers of about 100 other ethnic groups. Most Russians live in European Russia, in the west of the country. Inuits are among the groups in the frozen far north. People in different areas feel strongly about their own identity. Some former Russian republics became independent in 1991 and there are still people in other parts of Russia who would like to break away from the mother state. One such area is Chechnya, with its capital at Groznyy, where a revolt broke out in 1994.

Three quarters of the population lives in towns and cities. Russian cities have huge populations, so many people live in crowded high-rise apartment blocks. Moscow has one of the highest population counts in the world – over eight million people have made their homes here.

During the years of communism education was made a top priority by the government, but religious worship and freedom of speech were severely restricted. With the end of communism Russian believers began to worship more openly.

Russia's strong artistic tradition has produced many famous writers, composers, artists and musicians. From the 1800s onwards the country was a world leader in literature, music, drama, ballet and other arts. It has also become a leading medal-winner in the world of sport. This is actively encouraged by the government, which provides a wide range of sports facilities such as stadiums.

Ukrainian nuclear power station

The world's worst nuclear accident occurred in Chernobyl, north of Kiev, Ukraine, in 1986. Since then, many Ukrainians have opposed the use of nuclear power.

Moldova

Moldovans dress in traditional costumes to celebrate their country's independence in 1991. Moldovan customs and traditions were suppressed under communist rule .

The western states

Ukraine, Moldova and Belarus lie in Europe. They gained independence in 1991 after the collapse of the Soviet Union. Now they belong to the Commonwealth of Independent States, an alliance of former Soviet states.

These countries have wide plains, forested hills and many rivers. Fertile black soil covers much of the area, which has warm summers and mild winters. This makes the land suitable for farming and agriculture is very important to the economy. Crops include sunflowers (for vegetable oil), maize, wheat, tobacco and root vegetables. Fruits are grown for the canning industry and vineyards produce wine. Food processing is a major industry. Other industries include the manufacture of cement, machinery and clothes.

The Baltic states

Latvia, Lithuania and Estonia lie on the coast of the Baltic Sea in Europe. During the communist era many Baltic nationals were sent to labour camps in Siberia. Their languages and customs were suppressed. The Soviet Union took farms into state ownership and set up factories. Heavy industry has caused serious environmental damage. The Baltic states declared independence in 1991 when communism collapsed.

These are countries of low forested hills, lakes and streams. Crops include cereals, flax and potatoes. Cattle and pigs are also raised. Most people, however, live in cities and work in industry.

Dancers in Kazakhstan
● ●

Dancers wearing traditional costume perform to singing or the recital of an epic poem. They relive a heroic story from Kazakhstan's past.

St Anne's Church and the Church of the Bernardines are in Vilnius, Lithuania's capital. Religion was suppressed during the communist era. Today nearly all Lithuanians are Roman Catholics.

Armenia

Armenia is a rugged country in the Little Caucasus Mountains, with deep gorges, lakes and rushing rivers. Between the 1890s and the end of World War I the Turks massacred more than half a million Armenians and others were deported or fled. Over the years people from Armenia have settled in many other countries, including Israel. Today there are millions of Armenians living all over the world.

Most Armenians were farmers or herders until their country came under Soviet rule. The Soviets set up copper mines and factories and many Armenians moved to the cities to work. Today only a third of the population is rural, keeping sheep or cattle and growing fruit and vegetables. Most people speak the Armenian language, which is unlike any other and has its own alphabet. The country also has a strong artistic tradition that includes religious music and the making of decorative stone carvings called *khatchkars*.

Georgia

Forested mountains cover much of this land. The coastal lowlands have a mild climate and plenty of rain. Farmers grow citrus fruits, tea and tobacco. Farther inland cereals and vegetables are grown, as well as grapes for Georgia's famous wines. Georgia is noted for its food and hospitality and for the health resorts along its Black Sea coast. More than half the people live in cities and many work in food processing, the country's main industry.

Georgian horsemen

Georgian horsemen play a form of polo known as tskhenburi. Polo is a popular sport and most towns in Georgia sponsor a polo team.

103

Turkmenistan

Few people live in the arid desert region of Karakum that covers most of Turkmenistan. The inhabited areas of the country are mainly along the foothills of the Kopet Mountains in the south and in the river valleys in the southeast. Half the population of Turkmenistan makes its living from farming, which would be impossible without the canals that bring water from the rivers to irrigate the land. The most important crop is cotton, but grain, potatoes and grapes are also grown. Thoroughbred Turkomen horses and karakul sheep are reared and some farmers also breed silkworms. Wool is woven into the highly colourful carpets for which the country is famous.

Azerbaijan

In Azerbaijan the lofty Caucasus Mountains sweep down to the Caspian Sea. In the southwest a corridor of Armenian territory separates one section of Azerbaijan, called Naxçivan, from the rest. Much of the land is mountainous and through the broad valleys run the Kura and Aras Rivers, which provide

Tashkent
. . . .
The soaring modern television tower dominates the skyline of Tashkent, the capital of Uzbekistan. The city of Tashkent has always been a major crossroads and centre of communication and stands on the ancient Silk Road from China to the Middle East.

hydro-electric power for industry and irrigation for farming.

Azerbaijan was part of the Soviet Union until the Union broke up in 1991. The Russians brought heavy industry to the country and today the economy is based on Azerbaijan's large reserves of oil and natural gas. There are also many factories and over half the people live and work in towns and cities. In rural areas farmers grow cotton, fruit, tobacco and tea. Sheep and goats are herded on the mountain slopes.

Ownership of the Nagorno-Karabakh region has been challenged by neighbouring Armenia and there has been bitter fighting since the late 1980s.

Market in Tajikistan
. . . .
At an open market in Tajikistan shoppers buy melons grown in the fierce summer heat. The men wear traditional embroidered skull caps.

104

Uzbekistan

Much of Uzbekistan is a land of rolling plains and barren deserts, with the huge desert of Kyzylkum at its centre. Streams flowing from Kyrgyzstan's mighty Tian Shan Mountains water the fertile, heavily populated valley that contains the town of Fergana.

Uzbeks are nomadic herders by tradition, but the Soviet Union turned much of the country's grazing land into cotton plantations and the Uzbeks began to work on these. Uzbekistan became independent when the Soviet Union broke up in 1991.

Kazakhstan

Kazakhstan stretches from the salty Caspian Sea to the soaring Altai Mountains. In the north are high grassy plains called steppes and in the south there are sandy deserts. Kazakhstan has bitter winters and long hot summers.

For centuries the Kazakhs were nomads, roaming the plains with their herds of camels, horses, sheep and cattle. This traditional way of life changed when Russia conquered Kazakhstan about 100 years ago. The Russians began to mine iron and lead. They also planted the Kazakhs' grazing lands with wheat. When Kazakhstan became part of the Soviet Union rapid industrialization took place.

Many people in rural areas still live without electricity or running water. However, the discovery of oil in the Caspian Sea promises wealth. Independence in 1991 brought new pride in Kazakh traditions.

Turkmen carpet

A Turkmen woman works at the loom, weaving a carpet. Turkmen carpets have bold colours and a strong design.

Tajikistan

Tajikistan is a mountainous country, prone to earthquakes. In the Pamir Mountains snow makes the few roads impassable for more than six months a year. Yet in the fertile river valleys, where most people live, the summers are long and hot. Villagers grow mainly cotton, grain, vegetables, olives, figs and citrus fruits. Cattle breeding is important on the rich pasture lands. More and more rural people are moving to cities to find jobs in Tajikistan's textile factories, steel works and other industries.

Tajikistan was controlled by the Soviet Union from the 1920s. The Soviets built roads and schools, putting industry and agriculture under state control and discouraging religion. Independence came in 1991.

105

Estonia

Crowds of Estonians celebrate independence from the Soviet Union in 1991. They have gathered in Tallinn, their country's capital.

Kyrgyzstan

The early settlers of this mountainous country were nomadic peoples, who reared animals in the high valleys and took them down to graze in the warmer foothills during the bitterly cold winter months. Today only about half the population is rural, herding sheep, cattle, goats and pigs or growing cotton and tobacco. Most rural people are ethnic Kyrgyz and live in large clans, each with its own leader. A minority live in yurts. These wooden-framed, felt tents are traditional Kyrgyz homes, but today there might be a modern car parked outside them. One fifth of the people live in cities and work in industry.

Russia took over this country in the 1870s, bringing farm workers into the region. This left the nomads with fewer grazing grounds. Kyrgyzstan gained independence in 1991.

■ **RUSSIA**
Area: 17,075,000 sq km
Population: 148,366,000
Capital: Moscow (8,957,000)
Official language: Russian
Currency: Rouble
Main exports: Natural gas, petroleum, chemicals, machinery, timber, coal

■ **GEORGIA**
Area: 69,700 sq km
Population: 5,471,000
Capital: Tbilisi (1,283,000)
Official language: Georgian
Currency: Lary
Main exports: Food, chemicals, machinery, metal products

■ **ARMENIA**
Area: 29,800 sq km
Population: 3,732,000
Capital: Yerevan (1,283,000)
Official language: Armenian
Currency: Dram
Main exports: Chemicals, food products, machinery, metal goods

■ **AZERBAIJAN**
Area: 86,600 sq km
Population: 7,392,000
Capital: Baku (1,081,000)
Official language: Azeri
Currency: Manat
Main exports: Chemicals, food, machinery, oilfield equipment, petroleum, natural gas, textiles

■ **KAZAKHSTAN**
Area: 2,717,300 sq km
Population: 16,956,000
Capital: Astana (271,000)
Official language: Kazakh
Currency: Tenge
Main exports: Oil, metals, chemicals, grain, wool

Georgia   Armenia

Kyrgyzstan   Latvia

106

■ TURKMENISTAN
Area: 488,100 sq km
Population: 3,809,000
Capital: Ashgabat (411,000)
Official language: Turkmen
Currency: Manat
Main exports: Consumer goods, food, machinery, metals, oil, natural gas, cotton, textiles, chemicals

■ UZBEKISTAN
Area: 447,400 sq km
Population: 21,207,000
Capital: Tashkent (2,120,000)
Official language: Uzbek
Currency: Som
Main exports: Cotton, chemicals, food, metals, minerals, machinery, textiles

■ TAJIKISTAN
Area: 143,100 sq km
Population: 5,514,000
Capital: Dushanbe (592,000)
Official language: Tajik
Currency: Rouble
Main exports: Cotton, food, metals, textiles, fruit, vegetables

■ KYRGYZSTAN
Area: 198,500 sq km
Population: 4,528,000
Capital: Bishkek (642,000)
Currency: Som
Official language: Kyrgyz
Main exports: Food, machinery, manufactured goods, wool, chemicals

■ LATVIA
Area: 63,700 sq km
Population: 2,586,000
Capital: Riga (911,000)
Official language: Latvian
Currency: Lats
Main exports: Food, chemicals, manufactured goods

■ LITHUANIA
Area: 65,200 sq km
Population: 3,730,000
Capital: Vilnius (593,000)
Official language: Lithuanian
Currency: Litas
Main exports: Food, chemicals, manufactured goods

■ ESTONIA
Area: 45,100 sq km
Population: 1,517,000
Capital: Tallinn (503,000)
Official language: Estonian
Currency: Kroon
Main exports: Food, chemicals, manufactured goods

■ UKRAINE
Area: 603,700 sq km
Population: 52,179,000
Capital: Kiev (2,651,000)
Official language: Ukrainian
Currency: Hryvna
Main exports: Metals, machinery, food, chemicals, textiles

■ MOLDOVA
Area: 33,700 sq km
Population: 4,356,000
Capital: Chisinau (753,000)
Official language: Moldovan
Currency: Leu
Main exports: Chemicals, food, wine, machinery, textiles, tobacco

■ BELARUS
Area: 207,600 sq km
Population: 10,313,000
Capital: Minsk (1,634,000)
Official language: Belarussian, Russian
Currency: Rouble
Main exports: Machinery, transport equipment, petroleum, natural gas, chemicals, petrochemicals, food

Azerbaijan

Kazakhstan

Turkmenistan

Uzbekistan

Tajikistan

Lithuania

Estonia

Ukraine

Moldova

Belarus

ASIA

Some of the world's first great civilizations sprang up in Asia from 3500BC onwards. Their riches attracted trade and conquering armies. Over the centuries peoples such as the Mongols and the Turks built up and then lost vast empires. From the 1800s much of Asia was colonized by European countries. These new rulers took away wealth, but did not help the colonies develop. The original inhabitants stayed poor and were denied good education and job opportunities.

Tipu's tiger

This model of a tiger eating a European was made for Tipu Sultan of Mysore, India, in the late 1700s.

Great social changes have taken place in Asia during this century. Many colonies, such as India and Jordan, have become independent nations. In countries where a large majority of poor people were ruled by a wealthy few, communism seemed to be the answer. However, the spread of communism often caused war with capitalist countries. In 1991 the Soviet Union abandoned communism and, as it broke up, republics such as Kazakhstan and Uzbekistan became independent countries. Some Asian countries still have communist governments, although a number have recently held democratic elections for the first time.

Many Asian governments are now improving the economies of their countries by creating new industries and improving old ones. They are using both government money and foreign aid.

■ CONTINENTAL FACTS

Area: 44,387,000 sq km
Population: 3,381,282,000
  (excluding Russia)
Independent countries: 48
Highest point: Mount Everest
  (8,848 m), world's highest peak
Lowest point: Shore of the Dead
  Sea (393 m below sea level),
  world's lowest point
Largest lake: Caspian Sea
  (360,700 sq km)
Longest rivers: Yenisey (5,540 km),
  Yangtze (5,530 km), Ob (4,830
  km), Hwang Ho (4,830 km)

Russian women

In Siberia these Yakut and Khant women are making traditional clothes. Today these are worn only by rural people on special occasions.

Turkish mosaic

This portrait of the Emperor Justinian is made of mosaic (coloured glass cubes set in plaster). Justinian ruled the Byzantine empire during the AD500s. He made fair laws and promoted arts and learning.

109

China and its neighbours

RUSSIA

ULAN BATOR

MONGOLIA

KAZAKHSTAN

Altai Mountains

KYRGYZSTAN

• Urumqi

Gobi Desert

Baotou •

TAJIKISTAN

Taklimakan
Desert

Altun Mts.

Huang He

Taiyu

PAKISTAN

Kunlun Mountains

CHINA

• Lanzhou

Tibetan
Plateau

Chengdu •

Chongqing •

Chang Jiang Yan

INDIA

Himalaya

▲ Mt. Everest
8848m

Lhasa

Guiyang •

NEPAL

Mekong

Kunming •

Xi

BHUTAN

MYANMAR
(Burma)

VIETNA

LAOS

Giant panda

The giant panda lives in China's
southwestern bamboo forests. Its future is
threatened by the loss of this habitat and
by poaching. Efforts to breed giant pandas
in captivity in zoos around the world have
not proved successful.

| 0 | 200 | 400 | 600 | 800 | 1000 | 1200 Kilometres |
| 0 | | 200 | 400 | | 600 | Miles |

110

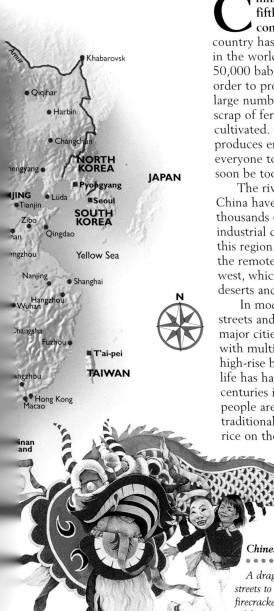

C hina occupies about one fifth of the Asian continent. This colossal country has the largest population in the world. Every day about 50,000 babies are born here. In order to provide food for such large numbers of people, every scrap of fertile land has to be cultivated. China currently produces enough food for everyone to eat, but there will soon be too many people to feed.

The river valleys of eastern China have been farmed for thousands of years and great industrial cities have grown up in this region. Fewer people live in the remote areas of the north and west, which include barren deserts and high mountains.

In modern times the narrow streets and low houses of China's major cities have been replaced with multi-lane highways and high-rise buildings. In contrast, life has hardly altered for centuries in rural areas. Most people are farmers and use traditional methods to cultivate rice on the terraced paddy fields.

Chinese dragon

A dragon is carried through the streets to the sound of exploding firecrackers during Chinese New Year celebrations. This festival is also celebrated in many overseas cities where people of Chinese descent have settled.

111

People and history

China has one of the world's greatest and most ancient civilizations, with a written history that stretches back over 3,500 years. Among its many inventions are the compass, fine porcelain, silk, gunpowder, paper, printing, and even banknotes.

During this century, China has experienced many changes.

After more than 2,000 years as an empire, the country became a republic in 1911. Following an uprising in 1949, China became a communist state. Since then the standard of living for most people has risen. Industrial modernization has continued and services such as up-to-date telecommunications networks have been developed.

■ **CHINA**
Area: 9,572,900 sq km
Population: 1,205,181,000
Capital: Beijing (7,500,000)
Official language: Mandarin
Currency: Yuan
Main exports: Crude oil, textiles, coal, grains, canned food, tea, fish products, raw silk, tungsten ore

■ **TAIWAN**
Area: 36,180 sq km
Population: 20,800,000
Capital: Taipei (2,720,000)
Official language: Mandarin
Currency: Taiwan dollar
Main exports: Electrical equipment, machinery, textiles, metal goods, plastic goods

■ **MONGOLIA**
Area: 1,566,500 sq km
Population: 2,371,000
Capital: Ulan Bator (575,000)
Official language: Mongolian
Currency: Tugrik
Main exports: Minerals, meat, hides, wool, livestock, consumer goods

■ **NORTH KOREA**
Area: 122,760 sq km
Population: 23,054,000
Capital: Pyongyang (2,640,000)
Official language: Korean
Currency: Won
Main exports: Coal, iron, copper, textiles

■ **SOUTH KOREA**
Area: 99,270 sq km
Population: 44,056,000
Capital: Seoul (10,628,000)
Official language: Korean
Currency: Won
Main exports: Machinery, electronic and transport equipment, manufactured goods, textiles, steel

■ **MACAU**
Area: 17 sq km
Population: 388,000
Capital: Macao
Official languages: Portuguese, Cantonese
Currency: Pataka
Main exports: Clothing, textiles, toys

■ **HONG KONG**
Area: 1,077 sq km
Population: 5,919,000
Status: This prosperous former British dependency became a Special Administration Region of China on 1 July 1997

China

Taiwan

Mongolia

North Korea

South Korea

dry to grow crops without irrigation. Also, expanding cities and factories have tended to spread across precious farmland. The people of China provide a large workforce, but as the population continues to grow more resources are needed for food, healthcare and education.

Towards a free market

China's farmers and workers had suffered centuries of injustice and poverty when the communists came to power in 1949 and attempted to improve their lives. In the 1950s and 1960s heavy industry was developed under state control. Farming was organized in communes, where villagers combined their land and farmed it together. From the 1980s free markets and private ownership were allowed in some areas. The economy boomed and Chinese goods were soon flooding all over the world.

Natural resources

China has rich resources of coal, oil, iron, tungsten, timber, hydro-electric power and fisheries. It is the world leader in rice and tobacco and its fertile farmland also produces large quantities of other crops including sorghum and wheat. It also has a centuries-old tradition of commerce, craft skills and invention. Despite all these advantages, the country has always had economic problems and still does today.

Many of its minerals are found only in remote, inaccessible regions. There are large areas of barren wilderness where it is too

Terracotta army
. . . .
The tomb of Emperor Shi Huangdi, who died in 210 BC, was guarded by an army of soldiers made out of terracotta.

N. and S. Korea – history

North Korea and South Korea formed a single country for hundreds of years, from the 1300s until this century. Between 1910 and 1945 Korea was occupied by Japan. This ended when Japan was defeated in World War II. After this the country divided into two, with troops from the USA occupying southern Korea and Soviet Union troops occupying the north. In 1950 North Korea attacked South Korea and millions were killed or made homeless. The war ended in 1953 but tensions between North and South Korea have continued.

N. and S. Korea – economy

North Korea is a communist country where all the factories, farms, even the cars, are owned by the government. The farms are collectives, where work and profits are shared. Most workers have jobs in factories. They cycle to work, leaving their babies in state-run nurseries.

South Korea has one of the world's fastest growing economies. Its industry is highly developed, producing computers and electrical goods. The country's rapid industrial growth has taken place since 1950. Before this its economy was based on farming. South Korea is a capitalist country. Its industry is privately owned.

Taiwan

Taiwan is an island off mainland China. One third of Taiwan's workers have jobs in manufacturing and it exports goods all over the world.

In the past, the island has been ruled by both Japan and China. In 1949, when China became communist, its defeated leaders fled to Taiwan and set up a government there. Tensions remain between anti-communist Taiwan and China.

Horse racing

Boys and girls as young as five take part in horse racing in Mongolia. Jockeys usually retire around age 12.

Hong Kong was loaned to Britain by China in 1842. It has become an important centre for trade, manufacturing and finance. Hong Kong was returned to China in 1997.

Mongolia

In the Middle Ages Mongolia built up one of the largest empires the world has ever seen under the leadership of Genghis Khan. When the empire fragmented, Mongolia was swallowed up by China. In 1924 it became a communist republic under the influence of the Soviet Union. Since the break-up of the Soviet Union in 1991, Mongolia has been a democracy.

By tradition Mongolians are herders. Mounted on stocky ponies they cross the country's bleak landscape of sand and gravel in seach of pasture for their sheep. Today, many have settled to work on livestock farms. Others have jobs in factories or mining.

Communist workers

There are many statues of heroic communist workers in North Korea. Since the country became communist in 1948 it has become heavily industrialized.

Macao

This view from Penha Hill shows the fourteenth-century temple, Ma Kwok, from which the colony takes its name.

115

Japan

Buddhist temple

Daigo-Ji is a Buddhist temple in the ancient city of Kyoto. Built of wood in the traditional Japanese style, it is set in a beautiful garden.

■ JAPAN
Area: 377,730 sq km
Population: 124,959,000
Capital: Tokyo (7,976,000)
Official language: Japanese
Currency: Yen
Main exports: Machinery, vehicles, ships, electronic equipment, steel, chemicals, textiles

Soya

Asah

Otaru
Sapporo

Hakodate

Aoi

Hachin

Akita

M

Honsh

Sea of Japan

Yamagata

Niigata

Koriyama

Shinano

Abukuma

Kanazawa

Toyama

Utsunomiya

Takasaki

Mit

JAPAN

TOKYO ■

Chiba

Yokohama

Mt. Fuji ▲
3776m

Nagoya

Shizuoka

Matsue

Kyoto

Okayama

Kobe

Osaka

Hamamatsu

Hiroshima

Takamatsu

Sakai

Wakayama

Kitakyushu

Matsuyama

Tokushima

Fukuoka

Kochi

Oita

Shikoku

Nagasaki

Kumamoto

Kyushu

Kagoshima

Miyazaki

NORTH PACIFIC
OCEAN

N

| 0 | 100 | 200 | 300 | 400 | Kilometres |
| 0 | | 100 | | 200 | Miles |

Tokyo Tower

* * * * * * * * * *

Tokyo Tower, built in 1958 to broadcast radio and television, sparkles against the night sky. At 333 m it is the tallest structure in Japan's capital city.

Hokkaido

Kushiro

The Japanese call their island country Nippon, meaning 'the source of the Sun'. This ancient name explains the red disc on their national flag, which represents the rising Sun. For many centuries emperors have been heads of state in Japan. Until the 1900s Japanese emperors claimed to be divine, believing they were descended from the gods. Today the emperor's role and duties are ceremonial only. Modern Japan is world famous for its powerful business corporations and advanced electronics technology. However, this is still a land in which traditions and ancient customs are held in the highest respect. Among the busy streets and bright lights of the capital visitors can glimpse the past in the form of temples and shrines. They can also take part in *chanoyu*, a 500-year-old tea-drinking ceremony that honours courtesy and hospitality.

Most of the population lives in crowded cities on the coastal plains. Inland are forested hills and mountains. The land is both beautiful and unstable. There are many volcanoes and earthquakes are common throughout Japan.

Kabuki *players*

* * * * * * * * * * * *

Actors in traditional costume and make-up perform a Japanese kabuki play. Men play both male and female roles and act out stories to music.

117

Economy

Japan is a land of economic miracles in both agriculture and industry. The country has only a small area of farmland, but yields of rice, tea, fruit and other crops are high. This is thanks to modern farming methods, which include growing specially developed high-yield crops and using fertilizers and pesticides. Modern equipment also means that fewer people are needed to work the land.

These small islands have become one of the world's greatest industrial powers. They have achieved this with hard work and investment in new technology. Japan has to import huge amounts of oil and raw material for industry, but it produces more cars and colour televisions than any other country. Japanese firms have expanded to open factories all over the world.

Large companies demand great loyalty from their staff. Employees may be expected to sing a special company song, wear a company uniform and join in daily physical exercise sessions. In return, many employers organize their workers' holidays, healthcare and housing.

Golf in Tokyo
• •

Players practise their swing in a three-tiered golf driving range in Japan's capital. Tokyo is densely populated with little open space, but this does not deter its golfers.

History

The Middle Ages was a time of turmoil. Power passed from a long line of emperors to warlords called shoguns. Sometimes there were civil wars between rival bands of warriors called samurai. From 1603 to 1867 Japan was united under shogun rule and closed its doors to the outside world. Then the emperors returned to power and opened up the country. A period of rapid industrialization followed.

During the 1930s the Japanese army invaded China. Then, during World War II, it overran most of Southeast Asia and the Pacific islands. Japan was defeated in World War II and occupied by United States forces until 1952. Since the 1950s the war-damaged economy has grown rapidly and today Japan is a major world economic power.

Geography

Japan is made up of about 3,000 islands. They are the tops of a huge mountain range that rises from the Pacific Ocean. Its rocks are still on the move, and sometimes this causes volcanic eruptions, earthquakes or huge waves called *tsunamis*.

Most Japanese live on the four largest islands, even though much of the land is taken up by towering mountains and forested hills. Streams and waterfalls tumble through deep gorges in this spectacular landscape.

On the coastal lowlands some of the most crowded cities on Earth spread on to land reclaimed from the sea.

Tokyo fish market
● ● ● ● ● ● ● ● ● ● ● ●

A woman buys octopus in Tokyo. Japan is a leading fishing nation and most Japanese eat fish every day.

South-east Asia

N

0 250 500 750 Kilometres
0 100 200 300 400 Miles

CHINA

MYANMAR (Burma)

Hanoi
Haiphong

Chiang Mai

LAOS
Vientiane

THAILAND

Da Nang

Bangkok

CAMBODIA

VIETNAM
Nha Trang

Phnom Penh

Ho Chi Minh City

Gulf of Thailand

South China Sea

Luzon

Manila

PHILIPPIN

Cebu

Sulu Sea

Minda

Zamboanga

Celebes Sea

Bandar Seri Begawan

BRUNEI

EASTERN MALAYSIA

Borneo

Ipoh

MALAYSIA

Kuala Lumpur

Medan

SINGAPORE

Batanghari

Pontianak

Kapuas

Balikpapan

Padang

Sumatra

Jambi

Sulawesi (Celebes)

Palembang

Barito

Banjarmasin

Java Sea

INDONESIA

Jakarta

Ujung Pandang

Bandung Java Surabaya

Malang Bali

Flores

Timor Sea

Javanese puppets

Javanese puppets are made of painted leather. The puppeteer moves them with rods and wires to enact the traditional folk tales of Java.

Southeast Asia has forested mountains, broad river valleys, low plains and palm-fringed beaches. Its tropical climate, fertile soil and plentiful monsoon rains make it ideal rice-growing country. The economy depends largely on agriculture. Most people live in villages, many in houses built on stilts, and work in the paddy-fields. Manufacturing industries thrive in the cities. The tiny nation of Brunei has become vastly wealthy since oil was discovered here in the 1920s.

All these countries except Thailand were once part of European empires. The Europeans established rubber, copra, palm-oil and banana plantations and developed the trade in spices. During this century the colonies gained independence, but this did not always bring peace. Many countries fell under military rule and oppression continues today.

Vietnam, Cambodia and Laos were involved in a major war.

The French ruled Vietnam until 1954, when communist guerrillas took over the north and the country was split into North Vietnam and South Vietnam. When communists tried to

Singapore

• •

Singapore is an island republic linked by bridge to mainland Malaysia. The country's wealth is based on shipping, banking, electronics and trade.

take over South Vietnam as well, North and South went to war. In 1965 the USA joined forces with the South against the communist North. Bitter fighting spilled over into Cambodia and Laos. The government of South Vietnam was overthrown in 1975. The US troops left and the country became one again in 1976. Vietnam's economy and environment suffered greatly as a result of the war. However, much has been done to repair the damage. Tourism and trade have developed steadily.

mor

Sculpture park in Laos

• • • • • • • • • • • • • • • • • • •

Buddha Park near Vientiane, the capital of Laos, features many Hindu as well as Buddhist sculptures. The park was built to honour both religions and their philosophies.

Indonesian gamelan

A gamelan is a collection of Indonesian musical instruments. It may include up to 40 drums, gongs, xylophones and chimes. Played all together, they make a magical tinkling sound.

Indonesia

Indonesia is the world's biggest archipelago, a long chain of more than 13,600 mountainous islands. Their many active volcanoes form part of the danger zone that geologists call the Pacific Ring of Fire. Indonesia has seen some of the most violent volcanic eruptions ever recorded. However, people continue to live close to the smouldering volcanoes because their ash makes the soil rich and fertile. The economy is based on agriculture, forestry and fishing.

Malaysia

Malaysia is a green land with mountains cloaked in dripping rainforest, huge plantations of rubber and oil palms and sandy beaches. Many Malays work growing rice and pineapples. Along the coast most people fish for a living. A large Chinese minority (35 per cent of the population) lives mainly in the cities. Malaysia has achieved economic success with rubber, tin and oil. Timber-felling has laid waste great areas of forest, but is now government controlled.

Malaysian satay

Small pieces of meat are skewered and barbecued over glowing charcoal to make satay. The dish is served with rice and peanut sauce.

Philippines

This island nation has many active volcanoes. Much of the land is clad in forest. Under the dictatorship of President Marcos the country suffered corruption, pollution and poverty. Marcos was overthrown in 1986. Today's government is working to solve the problems he left behind.

Rice terraces

The rice terraces of Luzon in the Philippines were dug out 2,000 years ago. Modern farming practices have increased rice production, but pesticides have damaged much of the land.

■ BRUNEI
Area: 5,770 sq km
Population: 276,000
Capital: Bandar Seri Begawan (46,000)
Official language: Malay
Currency: Bruneian dollar
Main exports: Crude oil, liquefied natural gas, petroleum products

■ SINGAPORE
Area: 640 sq km
Population: 2,874,000
Capital: Singapore City
Official languages: English, Mandarin, Malay, Tamil
Currency: Singaporean dollar
Main exports: Machinery, vehicles, electronic equipment, petroleum products, rubber, chemicals, food, clothes

■ PHILIPPINES
Area: 300,000 sq km
Population: 65,649,000
Capital: Manila (1,599,000)
Official language: Filipino, English
Currency: Philippino peso
Main exports: Clothes, electronic equipment, coconut oil, timber

■ MALAYSIA
Area: 329,580 sq km
Population: 129,239,000
Capital: Kuala Lumpur (938,000)
Official language: Bahasa Malaysia
Currency: Malaysian dollar
Main exports: Rubber, palm oil, timber, petroleum, tin, electronic equipment

■ INDONESIA
Area: 1,919,440 sq km
Population: 189,907,000
Capital: Jakarta (6,504,000)
Official language: Bahasa Indonesia
Currency: Rupiah
Main exports: Oil, liquefied natural gas, timber, rubber, coffee

■ CAMBODIA
Area: 181,040 sq km
Population: 9,308,000
Capital: Phnom Penh (800,000)
Official language: Khmer
Currency: Riel
Main exports: Rubber, rice, pepper, timber

■ LAOS
Area: 236,800 sq km
Population: 4,605,000
Capital: Vientiane (378,000)
Official language: Lao
Currency: Kip
Main exports: Timber, electricity, coffee, tin

■ VIETNAM
Area: 329,560 sq km
Population: 70,902,000
Capital: Hanoi (1,089,000)
Official language: Vietnamese
Currency: Dong
Main exports: Coal, iron, agricultural products including rice, rubber

■ THAILAND
Area: 513,120 sq km
Population: 58,584,000
Capital: Bangkok (5,876,000)
Official language: Thai
Currency: Baht
Main exports: Rice, tapioca, manufactured goods, machinery

Brunei

Singapore

Philippines

Malaysia

Indonesia

Cambodia

Laos

Vietnam

Thailand

India and its neighbours

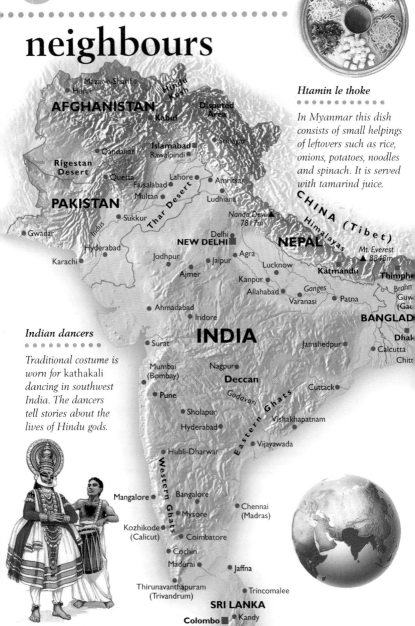

Htamin le thoke

In Myanmar this dish consists of small helpings of leftovers such as rice, onions, potatoes, noodles and spinach. It is served with tamarind juice.

Indian dancers

Traditional costume is worn for kathakali dancing in southwest India. The dancers tell stories about the lives of Hindu gods.

Map labels

AFGHANISTAN
Mazar-e-Sharif
Herat
Hindu Kush
Kabul
Disputed Area
Srinagar
Qandahar
Islamabad
Rawalpindi
Rigestan Desert
Quetta
Lahore
Amritsar
Faisalabad
Multan
Ludhiana
PAKISTAN
Indus
Sukkur
Thar Desert
Nanda Devi 7817m
CHINA (Tibet)
Gwadar
Delhi
Himalayas
Hyderabad
NEW DELHI
Agra
NEPAL
Mt. Everest 8848m
Karachi
Jodhpur
Jaipur
Lucknow
Katmandu
Thimphu
Ajmer
Kanpur
Allahabad
Ganges
Varanasi
Patna
Brahm
Guw
(Gau
Ahmadabad
Indore
BANGLAD
Surat
INDIA
Dhak
Mumbai (Bombay)
Nagpur
Jamshedpur
Calcutta
Deccan
Chitt
Pune
Godavari
Cuttack
Sholapur
Eastern Ghats
Hyderabad
Vishakhapatnam
Hubli-Dharwar
Vijayawada
Western Ghats
Mangalore
Bangalore
Chennai (Madras)
Mysore
Kozhikode (Calicut)
Coimbatore
Cochin
Madurai
Jaffna
Thirunanthapuram (Trivandrum)
Trincomalee
SRI LANKA
Colombo
Kandy
Galle

Indian well
· · · · · · · · · · · · · · · · · ·
Women collect water for cooking and washing from a well in the desert of Rajasthan, India. They carry it home in pots made of metal or clay balanced on their heads.

India is a land of contrasts. There are mountain ranges hidden permanently under ice and snow, plains crossed by broad rivers, a parched desert and tropical forests. Most Indians live in rural areas, where they grow rice and wheat and keep animals on small plots of land. Indian farms are getting smaller all the time, because under Hindu law, land is divided equally among the children on their parents' death.

In recent years thousands have moved to the cities to find work in industry. Heavy machinery and electrical goods are now manufactured alongside traditional products such as cotton and silk. Service industries such as tourism, education and communications are also growing in importance, as is the thriving film industry based in Bombay.

Afghan girl
· ·
This Afghan girl wears brightly coloured traditional dress and jewellery. She belongs to the Kyrgyz people of the far northeast.

Bangladeshi mothers
· ·
A healthworker in Bangladesh holds a clinic for mothers and babies. She may also advise on nutrition and food preparation.

Hkakabo ▲
5881m

JTAN

nphal

Mandalay

MYANMAR
(Burma)

Irrawaddy

Moulmein

■ Yangon
(Rangoon)

THAILAND

N

Buddhist monks process towards this beautiful gilded temple in the capital of Myanmar, Yangon, formerly Rangoon.

India's people and history

India has many ethnic groups, languages and religions. Most people are Hindu. According to Hindu tradition, people are born into social classes called castes. Strict rules govern the clothes, food and jobs of each caste.

In rural areas the way of life has not changed for centuries. In the cities people live crowded together in slums, while wealthier Indians choose a Western lifestyle.

India has seen the rise and fall of great empires founded on Buddhism, Hinduism and Islam. In 1858 India became part of the British empire. From the 1920s demands for self-rule grew with a peaceful campaign organized by Mahatma Gandhi. Independence finally came in 1947. Since then, the country has experienced conflicts over religion and language, but it has remained the world's largest democracy.

Afghanistan

Afghanistan has rugged, snow-capped mountains and scorching deserts. In summer, some Afghans roam the grasslands with their herds and sleep in tents of felted goat hair. In winter they settle to farm the valleys.

In the 1970s the Soviet Union became influential in Afghanistan and in 1979 Soviet troops invaded to support the left-wing government. Civil war then devastated the country. Soviet troops withdrew from Afghanistan in 1989, and in 1996 a Muslim group called Taliban (a word meaning 'students') controlled most of the country.

Pakistani potter

A potter adds the finishing touches to a teapot in Peshawar, Pakistan. Pakistan has a long tradition of fine craftwork, which also includes carpet making, leather tooling and metalwork.

■ MYANMAR (BURMA)
Area: 676,580 sq km
Population: 44,613,000
Capital: Yangon (formerly Rangoon, 2,459,000)
Official language: Myanmar
Currency: Kyat
Main exports: Teak, rice, pulses, rubber

■ AFGHANISTAN
Area: 652,090 sq km
Population: 20,547,000
Capital: Kabul (700,000)
Official languages: Pashto, Dari
Currency: Afghani
Main exports: Karakul skins, raw cotton, fruit and nuts, natural gas, carpets

■ INDIA
Area: 3,287,500 sq km
Population: 913,600,000
Capital: Delhi (8,400,000)
Official languages: 16 including Hindi, Bengali, Gujarati, Urdu
Currency: Indian rupee
Main exports: Gems and jewellery, clothes, cotton, textiles, tea, engineering goods

■ PAKISTAN
Area: 796,100 sq km
Population: 126,284,000
Capital: Islamabad (201,000)
Official language: Urdu
Currency: Pakistani rupee
Main exports: Cotton and cotton goods, rice, leather, carpets, fish

■ MALDIVES
Area: 300 sq km
Population: 238,000
Capital: Male (56,000)
Official language: Divehi
Currency: Rufiyaa
Main export: Fish

■ SRI LANKA
Area: 65,610 sq km
Population: 17,619,000
Capital: Colombo (588,000)
Official languages: Sinhalese, Tamil
Currency: Sri Lankan rupee
Main exports: Textiles, clothes, tea, gems, rubber, coconut products

■ BANGLADESH
Area: 148,390 sq km
Population: 122,210,000
Capital: Dhaka (6,106,000)
Official language: Bengali
Currency: Taka
Main exports: Jute, tea, hides, clothes, leather, newsprint, fish

■ BHUTAN
Area: 46,500 sq km
Population: 1,650,000
Capital: Thimphu (31,000)
Official languages: Dzongkha, English, Nepali
Currency: Ngultrum
Main exports: Timber and wood products, coal, rice, oranges and apples, distilled spirit, talc, cement

■ NEPAL
Area: 147,180 sq km
Population: 21,086,000
Capital: Katmandu (419,000)
Official language: Nepali
Currency: Nepalese rupee
Main exports: Grains, jute, timber, oil seeds, clarified butter, potatoes, herbs, hides

Myanmar

Afghanistan

India

Pakistan

Maldives

Sri Lanka

Bangladesh

Bhutan

Nepal

Pakistan and Bangladesh

Pakistan was once part of the British empire. When India won independence from Britain in 1947, two separate Muslim areas in northwest and northeast India became the country of Pakistan. Muslims from all over India moved to the new country while most Hindus stayed in India. In 1971 civil war broke out between East and West Pakistan, which split into two countries. The eastern half renamed itself Bangladesh, while the western half became modern-day Pakistan.

North Pakistan is a beautiful land of lakes and mountains. In the south is a sandy desert. In the centre is a great plain watered by the Indus River and its tributaries. A vast irrigation system allows the cultivation of wheat, rice and sugarcane. Pakistan's many industries produce cotton, carpets, sugar, metalwork and processed foods.

Most of Bangladesh is flat, very low-lying land. Two great rivers, the Ganges and the Jamuna, spill into a maze of waterways, forming the largest delta in the world. There are frequent floods, which have drowned livestock and people and washed away crops, causing famine. Most people live in villages and grow rice, sugarcane and jute, which is used to make ropes and matting.

Nepalese statue

This gilded statue of King Yoganendra Malla, a 17th century ruler of Patan in Nepal, stands in Patan's Durbar Square. A cobra rises behind the King.

Afghani bus

Open-topped trucks are used in Afghanistan for transporting people as well as goods. They are often beautifully painted and decorated by their owners.

Myanmar

Myanmar was called Burma until 1989. It is rimmed by mountains. Most people live in the delta of the Ayeyarwady (Irrawaddy) River and work in rice-paddies.

After independence from Britain in 1948, the country fell under harsh military rule. Objectors were shot or gaoled. In 1990 an election was held. The opposition party won, but the military continued in power.

Indian Ocean islands

The Maldives are a string of about 1,200 tiny tropical islands lying southwest of India. They are low and flat, many only just sticking up above sea level. Southeast of India is Sri Lanka, a large island ringed with palm-fringed beaches. It has a fertile plain that rises through rolling hills to misty mountains. Rainforest covers the southwest. About half the population are farmers, producing coconuts, rubber, rice and tea. A major source of the islanders' income is fishing, though tourism is the fastest growing industry.

Himalayan countries

Nepal and Bhutan lie in the Himalaya Mountains. The world's highest peak is Mount Everest in Nepal. Long-haired oxen called yaks are herded in the mountains, but most people are arable farmers, growing barley, citrus fruits and rice on the humid and fertile southern plains.

Tourism has boosted Nepal's economy, but it also threatens the environment. A cloud of pollution hangs over the capital, Katmandu. Trekkers and locals use timber for fuel and much of the country's forests have been cut down. Everyone is now encouraged to conserve resources.

In Bhutan, tourism and mountaineeering are limited.

Bhutani farmhouses
• •

In Bhutan traditional farmhouses cling to the mountainside above irrigated terraced fields. Villages are often isolated because they are cut off by the mountains.

Gathering sea salt
• •

In India salt-gatherers build low walls to trap the seawater when the tide comes in. When the water evaporates in the sun, salt is left behind.

The Middle East

I raq, Iran and Kuwait have vast expanses of desert. However, the discovery of oil has brought great wealth to these countries. Disputes over oil rights have also led to war.

Iraq and Iran are Islamic countries, governed by strict religious laws that deny many personal freedoms. Under Saddam Hussein, who came to power in 1979, Iraq invaded Iran. They fought from 1980 until 1988 over the Shatt al Arab Waterway, the important oil route that divides the two countries. Thousands were killed. In 1990 Iraq invaded Kuwait and claimed its territory. In 1991 Allied forces, including troops from the UK and USA, drove out the Iraqis. The Iraqis retaliated with bombs, setting hundreds of Kuwaiti oil wells on fire. Kuwait's economy was badly damaged and the land and sea polluted.

The Iraqi government has also persecuted the Kurds and the Marsh Arabs, many of whom have fled the country. Life is difficult for most other Iraqis because war has destroyed families, homes and jobs. Sanctions imposed by the United Nations have harmed the economy.

Iranian oil wells

Gas jets flame and black smoke fills the desert sky over the oil wells at Marun in Iran. Pollution is caused as waste gases are burned off the oil.

Yemeni Arab

Curved daggers called djambias are carried by most Yemeni men. The daggers have ornately carved handles made of ivory.

Klaicha

●　●　●　●　●　●　●　●　●　●　●　●

Klaicha *are small Iraqi pastries stuffed with dates and dusted with sugar. Date palms are widely grown in Iraq. Dates are also eaten in meat dishes.*

Mt Ararat ▲
5185m

ARMENIA

AZERBAIJAN

Aras

Caspian
Sea

TURKMENISTAN

● Tabriz

● Rasht

● Mashhad

● Mosul

Mt Damavand
5604m ▲

TEHRAN ■

AFGHANISTAN

● Kirkuk

Tigris

● Qom

Dasht-e Kavir

● Bakhtaran

IRAN

IRAQ

■ BAGHDAD

Zagros
Mountains

● Esfahan

Dasht-e Lut

● Karbala

● Yazd

An Nasiriyah ●

● Ahvaz

● Kerman

● Zahedan

Al-Basrah ●

● Abadan

● Shiraz

KUWAIT

■ Kuwait

● Bushehr

● Bandar Abbas

An Nafud

Persian Gulf

Strait of Hormuz

● Buraydah

BAHRAIN

■ Al Manamah

● Jask

Shaqra ●

QATAR

■ Doha

Dubai ●

Gulf of Oman

■ RIYADH

■ Abu Dhabi

■ MUSCAT

SAUDI
ARABIA

UNITED
ARAB
EMIRATES

▲ 3035m
Jabal Ash Sham

● Sur

Arabian
Sea

Rub al Khali
(Empty Quarter)

OMAN

N

▲ Jabal Sawda
3133m

● Salalah

SAN'A ■

Hadhramaut

INDIAN OCEAN

● Al Hudaydah

YEMEN

● Al Mukalla

| 0 | 100 | 200 | 300 | 400 | 500 | 600 | Kilometres |

| 0 | 100 | 200 | 300 | 400 | Miles |

Socotra (Yemen)

● Aden

Gulf of Aden

The Arabian Peninsula

The countries of the Arabian Peninsula are Saudi Arabia, Yemen, Kuwait, Qatar, United Arab Emirates and Oman. Bahrain is an island nation linked to the mainland by a causeway. Most of the peninsula is a desert where years pass without rain. Its only inhabitants are the Bedouin, who move with their camels between oases. Along the coast, people live by fishing or diving for pearls.

However, life has changed dramatically with the discovery of oil. Today the majority live in cities and work in the petroleum and construction industries. Profits from oil have been used to build roads and desalination plants that turn seawater into fresh water. Major irrigation systems enable some desert land to be farmed. New industries such as plastics and fertilizers are being developed. Oil money also provides free healthcare and other services including education.

Turkey and Cyprus

Turkey was once the centre of the mighty Ottoman empire, which lasted for 500 years, finally breaking up in 1920. Modern-day Turkey was established in 1923 by Mustafa Kemal. He abolished the Islamic legal system and gave women the vote.

In 1974 Turkey invaded Cyprus and forced the Greek Cypriots who lived in the north to flee to the south. The island remains divided, with continuing tension between Greek and Turkish Cypriots.

Fast food in Oman

A McDonald's sign advertises burgers at Muscat in Oman. Since the discovery of oil in the Middle East, Western corporations have rushed to sell their products to the Arab nations.

Krak des Chevaliers castle, Syria

This castle was built by the Crusaders in the 1200s. The Crusaders were European Christians who tried to recapture the Holy Land (Palestine) from the Arabs.

Turkish Cypriots

Village men relax in the sun outside a café in the north of Cyprus. They are playing tavala (the Cypriot name for backgammon). This dice game originated in Turkey and is popular throughout Turkish (northern) Cyprus.

Lebanon

Some of the people of Lebanon are Palestinian Arabs who believe that lands owned by Israel are rightfully theirs. The Palestine Liberation Organization (PLO) has been in conflict with Israel for many years and between 1969 and 1991 used Lebanon as a base for attacks on Israel. The country's Muslims and Christians have also had long-standing political differences. These, combined with the Palestine-Israel dispute, led to the outbreak of civil war in 1975. Troops from both Syria and Israel became involved and fighting continued until 1991. Some Israeli and Syrian troops remained in Lebanon to protect their countries' interests.

Turkish women
● ● ● ● ● ● ● ● ● ● ● ● ● ●

These Turkish women are spinning wool using short sticks called spindles. The wool fibres are twisted together to make a strong yarn.

Jewish call to prayer
● ● ● ● ● ● ● ● ● ● ●

The Jewish New Year festival of Rosh Hashanah begins with the blowing of a ram's horn. It calls people to make a new start and pray for past wrongs.

Israel

Israel is part of a historic land called Palestine. It was founded in 1948 as a home for the Jews. Since then, there have been bitter wars between the Jews and their Arab neighbours. The Arabs formed the Palestine Liberation Organization (PLO), believing that Israel's land belongs to them. In the 1960s Israel occupied Arab land on the Gaza Strip, the West Bank, the Golan Heights and the Sinai Peninsula. In 1994 peace was agreed between Israel and the Arabs, but tension continued.

Jordanian harvest

• •

Women pick the lettuce crop in the fertile valley of the river Jordan. The Middle East has little fertile land, but thanks to massive irrigation projects, some areas of desert can now be farmed.

Syria and Jordan

Syria and Jordan were two of the leaders of Arab opposition to their Jewish neighbour Israel. In 1967 Israel occupied Syria's territory in the Golan Heights, and the West Bank, formerly in Jordan.

Syria is undergoing rapid industrialization. Many people are moving to the towns in search of jobs in the developing textile and chemical industries. About half the people still live in farming villages along the coast, in the fertile river valleys and on the grassy western plains, where they grow cotton, fruit and vegetables.

Most Jordanians live in towns and cities. Many work for the government or in service industries such as finance, trade and tourism. Much of the land is rock or desert, so there is little large-scale agriculture. However, vegetables and citrus fruits are grown in the Jordan River valley.

■ **CYPRUS**
Area: 9,250 sq km
Population: 723,000
Capital: Nicosia (167,000)
Official languages: Greek, Turkish
Currency: Cyprus pound
Main exports: Clothes, shoes, wine, potatoes, citrus fruit

■ **TURKEY**
Area: 779,450 sq km
Population: 58,775,000
Capital: Ankara (3,023,000)
Official language: Turkish
Currency: Turkish lira
Main exports: Textiles, iron, steel, tobacco, fruit, leather clothing

■ **SYRIA**
Area: 185,180 sq km
Population: 13,393,000
Capital: Damascus (1,497,000)
Official language: Arabic
Currency: Syrian pound
Main exports: Petroleum and petroleum products, cotton, natural phosphate, fruit and vegetables

■ **LEBANON**
Area: 10,450 sq km
Population: 2,901,000
Capital: Beirut (1,500,000)
Official language: Arabic
Currency: Lebanese pound
Main exports: Clothes, jewellery, fruit

■ **ISRAEL**
Area: 21,950 sq km
Population: 5,256,000
Capital: Jerusalem (557,000)
Official language: Hebrew, Arabic
Currency: Shekel
Main exports: Fruit, vegetables, oil products, chemical products

Turkey

Syria

Kuwait

Saudi Arabia

■ JORDAN
Area: 91,880 sq km
Population: 4,440,000
Capital: Amman (1,272,000)
Official language: Arabic
Currency: Jordan dinar
Main exports: Phosphate, potash, fertilizers, fruit and vegetables

■ IRAQ
Area: 438,320 sq km
Population: 19,918,000
Capital: Baghdad (3,850,000)
Official language: Arabic
Currency: Iraqi dinar
Main exports: Petroleum, wool, dates

■ IRAN
Area: 1,648,000 sq km
Population: 63,180,000
Capital: Tehran (6,043,000)
Official language: Farsi
Currency: Rial
Main exports: Petroleum, carpets, fruit, cotton, textiles, metalwork

■ KUWAIT
Area: 17,820 sq km
Population: 1,433,000
Capital: Kuwait City (32,000)
Official language: Arabic
Currency: Kuwaiti dinar
Main export: Petroleum

■ SAUDI ARABIA
Area: 2,200,000 sq km
Population: 16,472,000
Capital: Riyadh (1,500,000)
Official language: Arabic
Currency: Riyal
Main exports: Petroleum and petroleum products, wheat, dates

■ YEMEN
Area: 531,000 sq km
Population: 12,302,000
Capital: San'a (500,000)
Official language: Arabic
Currency: Yemeni riyal
Main exports: Petroleum products, cotton, fish

■ OMAN
Area: 309,500 sq km
Population: 1,697,000
Capital: Muscat (380,000)
Official language: Arabic
Currency: Omani rial
Main exports: Petroleum, fish

■ UNITED ARAB EMIRATES
Area: 83,660 sq km
Population: 1,206,000
Capital: Abu Dhabi (363,000)
Official language: Arabic
Currency: Dirham
Main exports: Petroleum, natural gas, fish, dates

■ QATAR
Area: 11,440 sq km
Population: 559,000
Capital: Doha (236,000)
Official language: Arabic
Currency: Qatari riyal
Main exports: Petroleum, fertilizers

■ BAHRAIN
Area: 690 sq km
Population: 521,000
Capital: Al Manamah (152,000)
Official language: Arabic
Currency: Bahraini dinar
Main exports: Petroleum, aluminium products, manufactured goods, machinery, transport equipment

Lebanon Israel Jordan Iraq Iran

Yemen Oman United Arab Emirates Qatar Bahrain

AFRICA

■ CONTINENTAL FACTS
Area: 30,319,000 sq km
Population: 697,000,000
Independent countries: 53
Highest point: Mt Kilimanjaro (5,895 m)
Lowest point: Lake Assal in Djibouti (155 m below sea level)
Largest lake: Lake Victoria (69,484 sq km)
Longest rivers:
Nile (6,670 km),
Zaire (4,828 km),
Niger (4,184 km)

The map of Africa shows over 50 countries. Just 50 years ago most were ruled by powerful European nations, which became rich from mining and farming their colonies. From the 1960s African nations began to regain independence. However, the years of foreign rule had left most Africans poor, and without education or training. Colonial rule had often set one people against another and traditional homelands had been divided by new national borders. Trying to unite nations where people spoke many different languages and followed different religions was a hard task.

Many countries suffered years of dictatorship and millions became refugees from war, drought and famine. White South Africans refused to give the vote to the black people who made up most of this nation's population. However, in 1994 hope was brought to the continent when Nelson Mandela became South Africa's first black president. In the 1990s many African countries started holding democratic elections and looking towards a more peaceful future.

Berber water-seller

A familiar sight in Morocco, the water-seller offers cool drinks from his goatskin bag.

Yamoussoukro Cathedral

This 158 m high Roman Catholic cathedral is at Yamoussoukro in Côte d'Ivoire. The Basilica of Our Lady of Peace cost millions of dollars and was completed in 1989.

Zairean women
• • • • • • • • • • • • • • • •

Zairean women braid each other's hair
into many tiny plaits, adding beads. These
styles take hours to create.

Dr Livingstone window
• •

This cathedral window from Malawi
celebrates Dr David Livingstone, the
famous Scottish missionary. He explored
Malawi in the 1850s, campaigning
against slavery.

North Africa

North Africa is mainly desert, yet around 200 million people live here. The people of the north are of mixed Berber and Arab descent. Arab conquerors invaded in the AD600s and converted the original Berber inhabitants to Islam. Over the centuries, the two peoples intermarried, but they still form separate cultural groups.

The eastern peoples of Egypt and Sudan are descended from Nubians and Arab traders who settled the region. One of the world's greatest civilizations developed in the Nile Valley. The Ancient Egyptians were brilliant architects and engineers who built huge temples, tombs and towns. They studied the stars and worshipped many different gods. Their belief in life after death led them to preserve the bodies of their dead as mummies.

Powerful empires

The powerful Ghana, Mali and Songhai empires flourished south of the Sahara during the Middle Ages. Their wealth came from trade in gold, ivory and slaves.

Before independence around 50 years ago, most North African countries were controlled by

France, and their people still speak French today. Morocco was controlled by France and Spain, Libya by Italy, Egypt by Britain, and Sudan by Britain and Egypt. Ethiopia, with one of the oldest civilizations in Africa, has always managed to hold on to its independence.

Mask of Tutankhamun

This is the gold mask of Tutankhamun, a young Egyptian pharaoh (king) who died around 1340BC. It was discovered by British archaeologists in 1922.

SPAIN
Tangier
Rabat
Casablanca
MOROCCO
Marrakech
Oran A
CANARY Is.
Ifni
Ghardaï
ALGERI
In S
WESTERN SAHARA
S a
Mt.Tah
2818
MAURITANIA
MALI
Ah
Nouakchott
Timbuktu
Kaédi
Sénégal
Niger
SENEGAL
Niamey
Kayes
Ségou
GUINEA
Bamako
BURKINA FASO
BENIN
N

0   250   500   750   1000 Kilometres
0 100 200 300 400 500 600 Miles

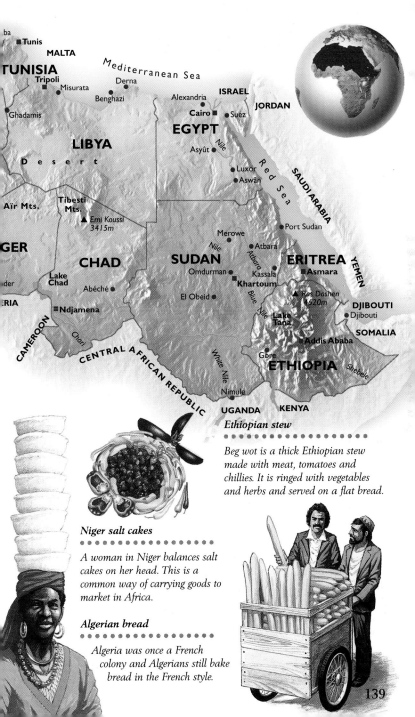

ba
■ **Tunis**

MALTA

TUNISIA
• **Tripoli**
• Misurata

Mediterranean Sea

Derna
• Benghazi

Alexandria
Cairo ■ • Suez

ISRAEL
JORDAN

• Ghadamis

LIBYA

EGYPT

• Asyût

Nile

D e s e r t

Luxor
• Aswân

Red Sea

SAUDI ARABIA

Aïr Mts.

Tibesti Mts.

▲ *Emi Koussi 3415m*

Merowe

• Port Sudan

GER

CHAD

Nile
• Atbara

SUDAN

ERITREA

YEMEN

der

Lake Chad

Abéché •

Omdurman •

Kassala

■ **Asmara**

RIA

■ **Ndjamena**

Khartoum

El Obeid •

▲ *Ras Dashen 4620m*

DJIBOUTI
• Djibouti

CAMEROON

Chari

CENTRAL AFRICAN REPUBLIC

Blue Nile

Lake Tana

SOMALIA

Addis Ababa

Gore
White Nile

ETHIOPIA

Shebele

Nimule

UGANDA **KENYA**

Ethiopian stew

• • • • • • • • • • • • • • • •

Beg wot is a thick Ethiopian stew
made with meat, tomatoes and
chillies. It is ringed with vegetables
and herbs and served on a flat bread.

Niger salt cakes

• • • • • • • • • • • • • • • •

A woman in Niger balances salt
cakes on her head. This is a
common way of carrying goods to
market in Africa.

Algerian bread

• • • • • • • • • • • • • • • •

Algeria was once a French
colony and Algerians still bake
bread in the French style.

139

Morocco   Western Sahara   Mauritania   Algeria   Tunisia

■ **MOROCCO**
Area: 458,730 sq km
Population: 26,069,000
Capital: Rabat (519,000)
Official language: Arabic
Currency: Dirham
Main exports:
  Phosphates, fertilizers,
  mineral products, dates,
  figs, canned fish, tobacco

■ **WESTERN SAHARA**
Area: 252,120 sq km
Population: 261,000

■ **MAURITANIA**
Area: 1,030,700 sq km
Population: 2,206,000
Capital: Nouakchott
Official languages:
  Arabic, French
Currency: Ouguiya
Main exports: Fish, iron
  ore, gypsum

■ **ALGERIA**
Area: 2,381,740 sq km
Population: 27,070,000
Capital: Algiers
  (1,507,000)
Official language: Arabic
Currency: Algerian dinar
Main exports: Oil, natural
  gas, olive oil, wine,
  machinery

■ **TUNISIA**
Area: 164,150 sq km
Population: 8,579,000
Capital: Tunis (597,000)
Official language: Arabic
Currency: Tunisian dinar
Main exports: Crude oil,
  fertilizers, phosphates,
  olive oil, textiles, fruit,
  fish products, machinery

■ **LIBYA**
Area: 1,759,540 sq km
Population: 4,700,000
Capital: Tripoli (858,000)
Official language: Arabic
Currency: Libyan dinar
Main export: Petroleum

■ **EGYPT**
Area: 1,001,450 sq km
Population: 56,488,000
Capital: Cairo
  (6,452,000)
Official language: Arabic
Currency: Egyptian
  pound
Main exports: Crude and
  refined oil, cotton, fruit

■ **SUDAN**
Area: 2,505,810 sq km
Population: 28,129,000
Capital: Khartoum
  (477,000)
Official language: Arabic
Currency: Sudanese dinar
Main exports: Cotton,
  gum arabic, sesame
  seeds, peanuts, sorghum

■ **CHAD**
Area: 1,284,000 sq km
Population: 6,098,000
Capital: N'Djamena
  (530,000)
Official languages:
  Arabic, French
Currency: Franc CFA
Main exports: Cotton,
  livestock, meat, hides

■ **NIGER**
Area: 1,267,000 sq km
Population: 8,361,000
Capital: Niamey
  (399,000)
Official language: French
Currency: Franc CFA
Main exports: Uranium,
  livestock, vegetables

■ **MALI**
Area: 1,240,190 sq km
Population: 10,137,000
Capital: Bamako
  (740,000)
Official language: French
Currency: Franc CFA
Main exports: Cotton,
  livestock, peanuts

■ **ETHIOPIA**
Area: 1,157,600 sq km
Population: 56,900,000
Capital: Addis Ababa
  (1,700,000)
Main language: Amharic
Currency: Ethiopian birr
Main exports: Coffee,
  hides, pulses, oil seeds

■ **ERITREA**
Area: 93,680 sq km
Population: 3,500,000
Capital: Asmara
  (368,000)
Official language:
Currency: Nafka
Main exports: Hides,
  cement, salt, gum arabic,
  citrus fruit

Libya

Egypt

Sudan

Chad

Niger

Mali

Ethiopia

Eritrea

Geography

North Africa is dominated by the world's largest desert, the Sahara. This scorching wilderness crossed by camel trains is bordered to the north by the fertile Mediterranean coast. In the northwest, the Atlas Mountains rise up, causing enough winter rain to grow crops such as wheat, grain, citrus fruit and olives. To the south of the Sahara Desert is a hot, dusty region called the Sahel. Here, nomadic peoples herd their animals across the thin scrub in search of pasture. In the east, the river Nile, carrying water from central Africa, has provided a lifeline through the shifting sands of Egypt for thousands of years. The Nile has been dammed at Aswan to produce hydro-electric power. Beyond this great river in the southeast are the relatively cool mountains of the Ethiopian Highlands.

Libyan mosques

Mosques rise above the skyline of Tripoli. Libya's capital has grown since the oil boom of the 1970s to house workers from the countryside.

Sudanese harvest

A woman sorts gum arabic into a basket. Gum arabic is produced by a type of acacia tree, and used in the manufacture of pills and paints.

Malian Muslims

Traders and travellers collect outside the Great Mosque at Djenné. Most Malians are Muslims. Mali has been a centre of Islam since AD1324.

Way of life

Many North Africans have moved to towns to work in factories or mines. Yet nomadic peoples such as the Bedouin and the Tuareg still live in the Sahara Desert by trading and herding camels and goats. They sleep in tents of animal hides. Some have settled at oases scattered across the desert. Farmers thrive along the Mediterranean coast, but others have been left starving and homeless by droughts that have made the land unproductive.

Economy

Libya has the richest economy in North Africa, based on its reserves of oil. The government has used profits from oil to improve farmland and to pipe water supplies across the desert. New industries have been developed, including mining and food processing. Mining boosts the economy in other North African countries, too. Oil and gas are mined in Algeria, phosphates in Tunisia and Morocco, iron ore and copper in Mauritania and uranium in Niger.

Farming occupies little land but many people. Algeria and Tunisia produce citrus fruits and olives, cotton is a valuable export crop in Egypt, and coffee grows in the cool mountains of Ethiopia. Many North African farmers use wooden ploughs pulled by oxen to prepare the land for sorghum, teff and maize, which are the main food grains. It is often a struggle to survive because of the severe droughts that plague these countries.

Tourism is increasingly important in Morocco, Tunisia and Egypt. Visitors come to enjoy the sun and ancient monuments.

A ruined city in Algeria
● ●

Ruined columns at Djemula, near Sétif, date back 2,000 years. At this time Algeria formed part of the fertile Roman province of Numidia.

Roman colosseum in Tunisia
● ●

The ruined colosseum of El Jem is a reminder that Tunisia was once part of the Roman empire. Chariot races and savage fights were staged here.

Lake Chad
● ●

Lake Chad is vital to the poor country of Chad. Camels that have travelled long distances across the desert can drink here and the deep waters are rich in fish.

The Suez Canal

The 160-kilometre Suez Canal was completed in 1869. It enables ships to pass directly from the Mediterranean Sea to the Gulf of Suez instead of sailing all the way round Africa. In 1956 Egypt's President Nasser nationalized the canal and as a result Egypt was attacked by Israel, Britain and France. The canal was closed from 1967 to 1975 because of further wars with Israel. Today Egypt is enlarging the canal to take big oil tankers and boost its revenue.

Sudanese school

Schoolchildren in central Sudan listen attentively to their teacher. Education in the south of the country has been disrupted for decades because of the civil war between Muslims and Christians.

The River Nile

Nearly all Egyptians live on the narrow strip of land watered by the river Nile. This is the only fertile land in Egypt and covers less than six per cent of its territory. Heavy rains at the source of the Blue Nile in Ethiopia make the river flood each year, leaving behind rich black mud ideal for growing crops. Since 1970, the floods have been controlled by the Aswan Dam, which produces hydro-electricity. However, the dam has also brought problems. The changes that it has made to the river's silt content have led to the erosion of the Mediterranean coast and to less fertile farmland.

Aswan High Dam, Egypt

The Aswan High Dam controls the floodwaters of the Nile. It has also silted up Lake Nasser, robbing farmland along the Nile of valuable nutrients.

143

West Africa

MAURITANIA

Senegal

SENEGAL
■ Dakar

GAMBIA
Banjul ■

Bissau ■
GUINEA-BISSAU   **GUINE**

Conakry ■

Freetown ■
SIERRA LEONE

Monrovia ■
LIBER

The culture of this region stretches back to the ancient empires of West Africa, such as Ghana, Mali and Songhai, which thrived between the AD500s and the 1500s. As these empires declined, smaller, independent kingdoms grew up. Then in the 1400s Portuguese traders arrived, and were soon joined by the British, French and Dutch. Over the next 400 years waves of Europeans invaded and set up colonies. They exploited the people and the land, establishing gold mines and plantations growing coffee, cocoa, sugar and cotton, and forcing the Africans to work on them as slaves. They also shipped Africans out to the Americas, where they were sold as slaves to other plantation owners. Many Africans died on the way, or did not survive the harsh life of slavery.

African elephant

The African elephant has long been killed in large numbers so that its tusks can be taken for the ivory trade. Today it is an endangered species.

Towards democracy

Slavery, the cruel trade in human beings, was abolished by Britain in 1807, but independence was slow to come. The colonial powers did not leave West Africa until the mid-1900s. Since then, some countries have known periods of military rule and dictatorship. Colonialism left most West Africans without education or training. Conflicts often developed between ethnic groups. Today education is improving and many countries are now democracies.

Voodoo queens

Cameroon's voodoo queens, who practise traditional spells and healing, sway during a ritual dance. Belief in the spirit world is widespread in the countries of West Africa.

Map of West and Central Africa showing:

BURKINA FASO — Ouagadougou

NIGER

NIGERIA — Kano, Kaduna, Benue, Niger, Ibadan, Abuja, Lagos, Port Harcourt

CÔTE D'IVOIRE — noussoukro, djan

GHANA — Accra

TOGO — Lomé

BENIN — Porto Novo

CHAD

CENTRAL AFRICAN REPUBLIC

CAMEROON — Douala, Yaoundé

BIOKO

EQUATORIAL GUINEA — Mbini

SÃO TOMÉ AND PRINCIPE

GABON — Libreville

CONGO — Brazzaville

DEMOCRATIC REPUBLIC OF CONGO

ANGOLA

Scale: 0 250 500 750 1000 Kilometres / 0 100 200 300 400 500 600 Miles

N (compass rose)

Way of life

In the towns of West Africa, people live in modern high-rise homes, or in wooden houses with tin roofs. Many townswomen travel to rural areas each day to work on small farms or help raising poultry or pigs. In the coastal lagoons villages of thatched huts are built on stilts in the water. The fishermen and traders who live there travel in canoes. Most West Africans live in mud huts in rural areas and are relatively poor farmers or herders. They grow millet, cassava and rice for food. Cotton, peanuts and palm-oil are grown as cash crops. Some workers operate modern machinery on rubber plantations owned by foreign companies.

Cotton plant

Cotton grows well in a tropical climate watered by heavy summer rain. The plants produce round bolls, which contain the soft white fibres used to make cotton fabric.

The harsh terrain and humid climate make farming difficult, yet the land holds priceless treasure. Nigeria is one of the world's major oil producers. Its oilfields are operated by foreign companies, which take about half the profits, with Nigeria receiving the remainder. Elsewhere in the region phosphates are mined for use in fertilizers. Huge deposits of diamonds, bauxite and iron ore promise future wealth.

145

SENEGAL
Area: 197,160 sq km
Population: 7,736,000
Capital: Dakar (1,382,000)
Official language: French
Currency: Franc CFA
Main exports: Fish products, peanuts, phosphates, chemicals

GAMBIA
Area: 11,290 sq km
Population: 1,026,000
Capital: Banjul (45,000)
Official language: English
Currency: Dalasi
Main exports: Peanuts and peanut products, fish and fish products, hides, palm oil

CAPE VERDE ISLANDS
Area: 4,030 sq km
Population: 395,000
Capital: Praia (62,000)
Official language: Portuguese
Currency: Cape Verde escudo
Main exports: Fish, salt, bananas

GUINEA BISSAU
Area: 36,120 sq km
Population: 1,028,000
Capital: Bissau (125,000)
Official language: Portuguese
Currency: Guinea-Bissau peso
Main exports: Fish, peanuts, coconuts

GUINEA
Area: 245,860 sq km
Population: 6,306,000
Capital: Conakry (706,000)
Official language: French
Currency: Guinea franc
Main exports: Bauxite, alumina, fruit, diamonds, coffee, hides

SIERRA LEONE
Area: 73,330 sq km
Population: 4,494,000
Capital: Freetown
Official language: English
Currency: Leone
Main exports: Bauxite, rutile, cocoa, coffee, diamonds, ginger

LIBERIA
Area: 99,070 sq km
Population: 2,640,000
Capital: Monrovia (425,000)
Official language: English
Currency: Liberian dollar
Main exports: Iron ore, rubber, timber, coffee, cocoa, palm oil, diamonds, gold

CÔTE D'IVOIRE
Area: 322,460 sq km
Population: 13,397,000
Capital: Yamoussoukro (2,534,000)
Official language: French
Currency: Franc CFA
Main exports: Cocoa, coffee, petroleum products, timber, fruit

GHANA
Area: 238,537 sq km
Population: 16,446,000
Capital: Accra (868,000)
Official language: English
Currency: Cedi
Main exports: Cocoa, gold, timber, bauxite, manganese, diamonds

TOGO
Area: 56,780 sq km
Population: 3,885,000
Capital: Lomé (500,000)
Official language: French
Currency: Franc CFA
Main exports: Phosphates, cotton, coffee, cocoa

BENIN
Area: 112,620 sq km
Population: 5,215,000
Capital: Porto-Novo (209,000)
Official language: French
Currency: Franc CFA
Main exports: Petroleum, cotton, cocoa, sugar, palm oil, peanuts, cement

BURKINA FASO
Area: 274,400 sq km
Population: 9,682,000
Capital: Ouagadougou (443,000)
Official language: French
Currency: Franc CFA
Main exports: Cotton, karite nuts, livestock, gold

NIGERIA
Area: 923,770 sq km
Population: 119,328,000
Capital: Abuja (306,000)
Official language: English
Currency: Naira
Main exports: Petroleum, cocoa, palm oil, rubber

Senegal

Gambia

Cape Verde Islands

Guinea Bissau

Guinea

Sierre Leone

Liberia

Côte d'Ivoire

146

Ghana

- **CAMEROON**
Area: 475,440 sq km
Population: 12,547,000
Capital: Yaoundé
  (750,000)
Official languages:
  French, English
Currency: Franc CFA
Main exports: Crude oil,
  timber, cocoa, coffee,
  peanuts, bananas, cotton

Togo

- **EQUATORIAL GUINEA**
Area: 28,050 sq km
Population: 379,000
Capital: Malabo (10,000)
Official language:
  Spanish
Currency: Franc CFA
Main exports: Cocoa,
  timber, coffee

Benin

- **SÃO TOMÉ AND PRINCIPE**
Area: 1,000 sq km
Population: 122,000
Capital: São Tomé
  (35,000)
Official language:
  Portuguese
Currency: Dobra
Main exports: Cocoa,
  copra, coffee, bananas,
  palm oil

Burkina Faso

- **GABON**
Area: 267,670 sq km
Population: 1,012,000
Capital: Libreville
  (350,000)
Official language: French
Currency: Franc CFA
Main exports: oil,
  manganese, timber,
  uranium

Nigeria

- **CONGO**
Area: 342,000 sq km
Population: 2,441,000
Capital: Brazzaville
  (586,000)
Official language: French
Currency: Franc CFA
Main exports: Petroleum,
  timber, coffee, cocoa

Cameroon

Equatorial Guinea

São Tomé and Príncipe

Gabon

Congo

Geography

The coast of West Africa is fringed with mangroves and mudflats washed with warm rain blown in from the ocean. Inland, lagoons and coastal swamps give way to lush tropical rainforests that stretch hundreds of kilometres. Meandering rivers often provide the only form of transport, as the jungle encroaches on mud-built roads that get washed away in the rainy season. The steaming forests rise to cooler central highlands. Rivers here sometimes tumble from spectacular heights into deep gorges. During the rains they flood the land with fertile mud, occasionally washing away whole settlements of houses. Finally the landscape opens out into an interior of savanna grasslands that shimmer in the heat.

Togo dancers
. . . .

In Togo, traditional dancers wear horns, scarves and brightly coloured beaded kilts as they prepare for a ritual celebration.

Central and East Africa

The Democratic Republic of Congo (DRC) is crossed by the river Congo, which forms the country's chief means of transport. In the north, the humid climate supports a vast area of dense rainforest. To the south are open savannas. The government has set aside large areas of land as wildlife sanctuaries.

The river Congo offers massive hydro-electric potential, while the rocks conceal deposits of uranium and gold. DRC is a world leader in the production of copper, cobalt and industrial diamonds, but most people are subsistence farmers. In 1996 tragedy struck twice for DRC. The world price of copper fell, causing poverty and hardship, and war broke out with Rwanda.

Uganda

Uganda's rich red farmland and equatorial climate support coffee, bananas, maize and millet. Uganda also has thick green forest, arid scrubland and beautiful lakes.

CABINDA (Angola)

Matadi

During the 1970s Uganda was ruled by General Idi Amin. Ugandan Asians were expelled, businesses collapsed and Amin's political opponents were murdered. Amin was overthrown in 1979. Ugandan governments since then have worked to unite the country and repair its economy.

Central African Republic

Central African Republic has high grassy plains and lush rainforest. In the rainy season roads become a sea of mud, so rivers are used for transport. Diamonds are mined and other exports are rubber, cotton and timber. Trade is mainly with France, which

Masai women

Masai women wear bright cloth and beaded collars for a ceremony in which their sons will become junior elders.

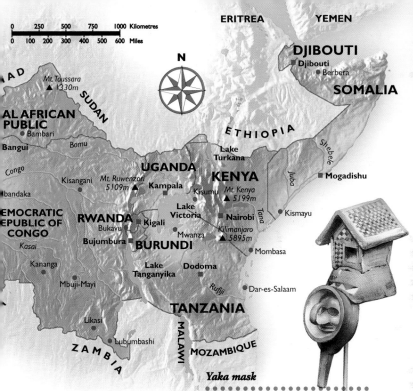

Yaka mask

. . . .

This carved mask is held over the face by Yaka boys during ceremonies to mark their passage into manhood. The Yaka people live in southern DRC.

Mogadishu

. . . .

These whitewashed buildings in Somalia's capital city and chief port are designed in the Arab style.

Djibouti

Somalia

Kenya

Tanzania

Uganda

■ DJIBOUTI
Area: 23,200 sq km
Population: 481,000
Capital: Djibouti (317,000)
Official languages: Arabic, French
Currency: Djibouti franc
Main exports: Hides, livestock, coffee in transit from Ethiopia

■ SOMALIA
Area: 737,660 sq km
Population: 9,517,000
Capital: Mogadishu (1,000,000)
Official languages: Somali, Arabic
Currency: Somali shilling
Main exports: Bananas, livestock, hides

■ KENYA
Area: 582,650 sq km
Population: 28,113,000
Capital: Nairobi (1,104,000)
Official languages: Swahili, English
Currency: Kenya shilling
Main exports: Tea, coffee, fruit, petroleum products

■ TANZANIA
Area: 945,040 sq km
Population: 28,783,000
Capital: Dodoma (204,000)
Official languages: Swahili, English
Currency: Tanzanian shilling
Main exports: Coffee, cotton, sisal, cloves, tobacco

■ UGANDA
Area: 241,040 sq km
Population: 19,246,000
Capital: Kampala (774,000)
Official language: English
Currency: Uganda shilling
Main exports: Coffee, cotton, tea, tobacco

■ RWANDA
Area: 26,340 sq km
Population: 7,789,000
Capital: Kigali (157,000)
Official languages: Kinyarwanda, French
Currency: Rwanda franc
Main exports: Coffee, tea, tin

■ BURUNDI
Area: 27,830 sq km
Population: 5,985,000
Capital: Bujumbura (236,000)
Official languages: Kirundi, French
Currency: Burundi franc
Main exports: Coffee, tea, bananas

■ DEMOCRATIC REPUBLIC OF CONGO
Area: 2,344,880 sq km
Population: 41,166,000
Capital: Kinshasa (3,804,000)
Official language: French
Currency: Congo franc
Main exports: Copper, coffee, diamonds, cobalt, petroleum

■ CENTRAL AFRICAN REPUBLIC
Area: 622,440 sq km
Population: 3,258,000
Capital: Bangui (452,000)
Official language: French
Currency: Franc CFA
Main exports: Coffee, diamonds, timber, cotton, tobacco

Rwanda

Burundi

Dem. Republic of Congo

Central African Republic

Mandrill
● ●

Mandrills are large monkeys related to baboons. They are powerful animals with colourful faces and buttocks that live in small family groups in the rainforests of central West Africa. They climb trees to pick fruit and dig for roots and insects.

Rwanda and Burundi

The villages of Rwanda and Burundi cling to green, tropical hillsides. These countries have river valleys, grassland, volcanoes and swamps. Most people are farmers who herd goats and cattle and grow bananas, beans, maize and cassava. The majority belong to a group of people called the Hutu, but a minority are Tutsis.

For hundreds of years the Tutsis held power while the Hutus were poor peasant farmers. In the late 1890s Ruanda-Urundi (the two countries combined) became first a German, then a Belgian colony. After independence in 1962 Hutus gained power in Rwanda and years of violence against the Tutsis followed. Many fled to Burundi where Tutsis remained in control, suppressing Hutu uprisings. In 1994 the leaders of Rwanda and Burundi were killed in a plane crash, believed to have been

Tutsi dancers
. . . .
Tutsi men wearing plumed headdresses perform a ceremonial lion dance. Tutsis live in Rwanda, Burundi and DRC.

Tanzanian stew
. . . .
Tanzanian beef stew is made with coconut milk, tomatoes and plantains. Plantain is like banana, but needs to be cooked.

caused by terrorists. A bitter war between Hutus and Tutsis broke out in both countries. Millions of innocent people were killed and others fled as refugees to Tanzania and DRC. A major international relief effort was instigated to help both nations. In 1996 war broke out again between the Hutus and Tutsis of Rwanda and DRC.

Taxis in Kampala, Uganda
. . . .
Minibuses park in the market district of Kampala, Uganda's capital. They operate as shared taxis. Now roads have been repaired after long years of war, they offer a better service than the railways.

151

Kenya

Kenya is one of the most beautiful countries in Africa. The low coastal plain with its thick tropical forests rises to a broad grassland plateau. In the north is a parched desert and to the west are the ancient volcanoes and craggy cliffs of the Great Rift Valley. Tourists are attracted by the wildlife, the scenery, white beaches and luxury hotels, but few see the other side of Kenya. There is poor housing on the edge of Nairobi and labourers on coffee plantations and commercial farms are badly paid. Educational standards are high, but many people cannot find jobs. Unemployment increased when large numbers of refugees flooded in to escape the civil war in neighbouring Somalia.

Tanzanian carver

A Makonde carver works on a wooden sculpture. The Makonde people, who live on the coast and the Mozambique border are renowned for their skill at carving.

Tanzania

The snow-covered mass of Mount Kilimanjaro – Africa's highest mountain – looms high above northern Tanzania, close to the border with Kenya. To the west of Kilimanjaro are other natural wonders such as the Ngorongoro Crater, the centre of an ancient volcano inhabited only by elephants, rhinoceroses, hyenas and other wild animals. Vast herds of zebras, antelopes, wildebeests and the lions and cheetahs that prey on them roam the Serengeti Plains. Clouds of dust mark the passing of cattle and their Masai herders. The climate is cooler in the mountainous areas in the north and south of the country. The south also has the huge Selous Wildlife Reserve, one of the largest game conservation reserves in the world.

Tanzania's economy is based on agriculture, although two thirds of the country cannot be farmed because of lack of water and swarms of disease-carrying tsetse flies. The coastal region is fertile, producing bananas, mangoes, sugarcane and sisal. Other important crops are tea, coffee, tobacco and cotton.

Kenyan bottle

This beautifully decorated bottle has been made by a Kikuyu craftsman out of a gourd, a plant like a pumpkin. Kenyans are famed for their artistic skill.

Somalia

Somalia is a hot, dry country. Most Somalis are nomads who live by herding camels, sheep and goats. In the south farmers grow crops such as bananas, citrus fruits and sugarcane.

The north of the country was ruled by the British from 1884 and Italy controlled the south from 1905. These colonies were important because their ports lay on international shipping routes. They joined to become one independent nation in 1960.

Somalia is a poor country and it suffered from severe drought in the 1970s and 1980s. Nomadic peoples faced starvation when their herds died and in 1974 war broke out with Ethiopia. Somalia agreed a peace treaty with Ethiopia in 1988. But in the 1990s civil war between Somali clans led to thousands of deaths.

Well in Somalia

Children draw water from a well in Bardera, Somalia. Drinking water is vital to their survival, as Somalians have less to eat than any other people in the world.

Djibouti

Djibouti is mainly a wilderness of scrub and rock. The economy is dependent on shipping and the country is named after its capital city, a major port situated on important trade routes between the Gulf of Aden and the Red Sea. Djibouti has been the chief port for trade with Ethiopia since it was built by French colonists in the 1800s.

In the past most of Djibouti's people – two groups called the Afars and the Issas – were nomads, herding sheep, goats, camels and cattle in the deserts and mountains. Many still live in this way, but increasing numbers leave the countryside to seek work in the port. Some go even further, finding jobs in countries such as Saudi Arabia.

Somali bread

A Somali woman pours dough on to a griddle to make anjeera. This flat, unleavened bread is shaped like a pancake and eaten with stew.

153

Southern Africa

At the heart of this land is a high flat plateau of vast plains and bush. This is the savanna grassland. Parts of it have been turned into reserves for the protection of wild animals. This region is tropical, but the high altitude gives it a mild climate. In the west, much of Angola and Namibia is a sandy wasteland. The Namib Desert is one of the driest places on Earth. The Kalahari Desert spreads east into Botswana. At the tip of the continent is South Africa, a land of great scenic beauty dominated by the dramatic Drakensberg Mountains. In the east it is hot and humid, with tropical rainforest covering the lower land near the coast. The great rivers of southern Africa, including the Orange and the mightly Zambezi, are dammed to provide hydro-electric power and water for irrigation.

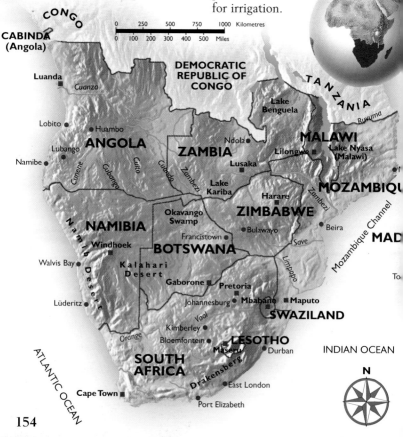

| 0 | 250 | 500 | 750 | 1000 | Kilometres |
| 0 | 100 | 200 | 300 | 400 | 500 | Miles |

CONGO

CABINDA (Angola)

DEMOCRATIC REPUBLIC OF CONGO

TANZANIA

Luanda
Cuanza

Lobito
Huambo
Lubango
Namibe

ANGOLA

Cunene
Cubango
Cuito

ZAMBIA

Ndola
Lusaka

Lake Benguela

MALAWI
Lilongwe
Lake Nyasa (Malawi)

Ruvuma

Zambezi

Lake Kariba

Harare

ZIMBABWE

Bulawayo

MOZAMBIQUE

Beira

MAD

Okavango Swamp

NAMIBIA
Windhoek

Francistown

BOTSWANA

Save

Zambezi

Mozambique Channel

Walvis Bay

Kalahari Desert

Gaborone

Pretoria

Limpopo

To

Lüderitz

Johannesburg
Mbabane
Maputo

Namib Desert

SWAZILAND

Kimberley
Vaal

Bloemfontein

LESOTHO
Maseru

Durban

INDIAN OCEAN

Orange

SOUTH AFRICA

Drakensberg

East London

N

Cape Town

ATLANTIC OCEAN

Port Elizabeth

154

History

In the 1800s diamonds and gold were discovered here and fortune-hunters began to rush in from Europe. The countries of Southern Africa were seized by Portugal, Germany, Britain, Netherlands and France. Hungry for wealth, the Europeans conquered the African peoples, or tricked them into selling mining rights. Thus the enormous riches yielded up by the land benefited only the white minority.

In 1950 the white government of South Africa, the richest country in the continent, introduced the policy of apartheid. This separated blacks from whites and refused them equal rights. The cruel regime left millions in grinding poverty. In 1994 democratic elections gave South Africa its first majority black government led by

South Africa's parliament
● ●

For more than a century, only whites were allowed inside South Africa's parliament. In 1994 South Africa became a multi-racial democracy.

President Nelson Mandela. His triumph brought hope to all the peoples of southern Africa, where the colonial past has left many with poor housing, inadequate education and limited job opportunities.

Ringtail lemur
● ● ● ● ● ● ● ● ● ● ● ● ● ● ● ● ● ● ●

This rare lemur is found only on Madagascar. It evolved when the island split from the mainland 160 million years ago.

ROS

● Antseranana

nga ●

● Toamasina

arivo
:AR

Delicious honeycomb
● ● ● ● ● ● ● ● ● ● ● ● ● ● ● ● ● ● ●

A San man from Botswana enjoys a honeycomb. To get the honeycomb, the San climb a tree and smoke out the bees. The bee grubs in the comb are considered the tastiest delicacy.

| Angola | Namibia | South Africa | Swaziland | Zimbabwe |

■ ANGOLA
Area: 1,246,700 sq km
Population: 10,276,000
Capital: Luanda
  (1,200,000)
Official language:
  Portuguese
Currency: Kwanza
Main exports: Crude oil,
  coffee, diamonds, fish
  products, sisal, maize,
  palm-oil

■ LESOTHO
Area: 30,350 sq km
Population: 1,882,000
Capital: Maseru
  (110,000)
Official language:
  Sesotho, English
Currency: Loti
Main exports: Wool,
  mohair, diamonds,
  wheat, vegetables,
  livestock

■ MOZAMBIQUE
Area: 799,380 sq km
Population: 15,322,000
Capital: Maputo
  (1,098,000)
Official language:
  Portuguese
Currency: Metical
Main exports: Shrimps,
  cashew nuts, sugar,
  petroleum products,
  copra, cotton

■ BOTSWANA
Area: 581,730 sq km
Population: 1,143,000
Capital: Gaborone
  (139,000)
Official language: English
Currency: Pula
Main exports: Diamonds,
  copper, nickel, meat and
  meat products, hides,
  textiles

■ SOUTH AFRICA
Area: 1,127,000 sq km
Population: 40,774,000
Capitals: Cape Town
  (2,351,000), Pretoria,
  Bloemfontein
Official languages: 11,
  including English,
  Ndebele, Afrikaans
Currency: Rand
Main exports: Gold,
  metals, diamonds, food
  products, machinery

■ SWAZILAND
Area: 17,360 sq km
Population: 814,000
Capital: Mbabane
  (39,000)
Official languages:
  English, Siswati
Currency: Lilangeni
Main exports: Sugar,
  wood and forest
  products, canned fruit,
  citrus fruit, asbestos

■ MADAGASCAR
Area: 587,040 sq km
Population: 13,259,000
Capital: Antananarivo
  (804,000)
Official languages:
  Malagasy, French
Currency: Malagasy franc
Main exports: Coffee,
  cloves, vanilla, sugar,
  sisal, shrimps

■ MALAWI
Area: 118,480 sq km
Population: 9,135,000
Capital: Lilongwe
  (234,000)
Official languages:
  Chichewa, English
Currency: Kwacha
Main exports: Tobacco,
  sugar, tea, cotton,
  peanuts

■ SEYCHELLES
Area: 455 sq km
Population: 72,000
Capital: Victoria (25,000)
Official languages:
  Creole, English, French
Currency: Seychelles
  rupee
Main exports: Copra,
  fish, cinnamon

■ MAURITIUS
Area: 2,040 sq km
Population: 1,098,000
Capital: Port Louis
  (144,000)
Official language: English
Currency: Mauritius
  rupee
Main exports: Sugar,
  clothing, tea, toys, games

| Zambia | Malawi | Mozambique | Madagascar | Seychelles |

Lesotho   Botswana

■ **ZAMBIA**
Area: 752,610 sq km
Population: 8,885,000
Capital: Lusaka
  (921,000)
Official language: English
Currency: Kwacha
Main exports: Copper,
  cobalt, zinc, emeralds,
  lead, tobacco

■ **ZIMBABWE**
Area: 390,580 sq km
Population: 10,898,000
Capital: Harare
  (657,000)
Official language: English
Currency: Zimbabwe
  dollar
Main exports: Tobacco,
  iron alloys, gold, nickel,
  cotton, steel

■ **NAMIBIA**
Area: 824,270 sq km
Population: 1,584,000
Capital: Windhoek
  (125,000)
Official language: English
Currency: Namibian
  dollar
Main exports: Diamonds,
  uranium, fish products,
  meat products, livestock

■ **COMOROS**
Area: 1,862 sq km
Population: 607,000
Capital: Moroni (22,000)
Official languages:
  French, Arabic
Currency: Comorian franc
Main exports: Vanilla,
  cloves, ylang ylang,
  copra, coffee

Comoros   Mauritius

Economy

Mining has always formed the backbone of the economy in southern Africa. The oldest known mines in the world are in Swaziland, where iron ore was mined 43,000 years ago. Diamonds are found in large quantities in the volcanic rocks of South Africa, which exports more of these precious gems than any other country on Earth. South Africa also has the world's biggest goldfield and considerable reserves of coal. Zambia's main export is copper, found near the border with DRC. Mines in the Namib Desert produce uranium, a highly radioactive metal used in nuclear power stations.

Cattle are reared on the grassy plains of South Africa, which also produces large quanitites of grapes and grain. Tropical fruits grow in the lush eastern lands. But arid conditions make farming difficult in much of this region.

Mauritian children
• • • • • • • • • • • •

A group of children from a fishing community show the mix of different peoples who live in Mauritius. They are the descendants of European settlers, Chinese and Indian traders and African slaves.

Fruits of Zimbabwe
• • • • • • • • • • • •

Mango, passion fruit, pineapple and avocado are four of the delicious fruits cultivated in Zimbabwe.

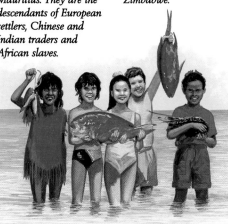

AUSTRALASIA

The isolated position of this continent, which includes Australia, New Zealand and the Pacific Islands, means that the wildlife found here is often very different from that in the rest of the world. The only two mammals in the world that lay eggs, the duck-billed platypus and the echidna (a spiny anteater), are found in Australia and New Guinea. These countries are also the home of pouched mammals called marsupials, which include kangaroos, wallabies, koala bears and wombats.

Australia's landscapes include desert, rainforest, eucalyptus woodland, muddy creeks and scrub. The climate changes from tropical in the north to temperate in the south. Low plateaus and plains, dotted with large expanses of scrub and desert, take up much of the land. New Zealand, which is made up of two main islands, is a mountainous country with hot springs and geysers in the north and glaciers in the south. Coconut groves and rainforests thrive on the Pacific Islands. Turtles, crabs and seabirds from the Pacific Ocean visit the islands' coral reefs and sandy shores.

Maori woodcarving

The Maoris came to New Zealand around AD800. They crossed the Pacific in wooden boats and developed the art of woodcarving with distinctive figures of gods and demons.

■ CONTINENTAL FACTS
Area: 8,510,000 sq km (95% of this is Australia and New Zealand)
Population: 28,000,000
Independent countries: 14
Largest country: Australia
Smallest country: Nauru
Highest point: Mt Wilhelm (4,694 m) in Papua New Guinea
Lowest point: Lake Eyre (12 m below sea level) in Australia
Longest rivers: Murray (2,575 km) and its tributary, the Darling (2,740 km), in Australia

Didgeridoo

Aboriginals today still play the didgeridoo, a traditional pipe made of tree branches that sounds very deep notes. The instrument is so long it has to be rested on the ground.

Polynesian harvest

Fruits and vegetables were taken from their east Asian homelands by the early Polynesian settlers on their voyages over the Pacific. Today these are important crops in the Polynesian islands.

Coconut

Yam

Tora

Breadfruit

Easter Island

About 600 strange stone heads were left behind on Easter Island by early Polynesian settlers. This island is owned by Chile, though it lies nearly 4,000 km off its western shores. The sculptures are around 1,000 years old.

The Pacific Islands

Most of the Pacific islands were formed by fierce volcanic activity, which continues today. Some islands, such as New Caledonia and the main islands of the Fiji, Samoa and Vanuatu groups, have steep, forested mountains. Others are low islands formed from corals, the tiny warm-water creatures that live inside chalky skeletons. Volcanoes that have collapsed into the water may be capped by a ring of coral growth called an atoll. This is made from coral remains that have built up around underwater mountains and ridges until they stick out above the sea. Both mountainous and low islands are often surrounded by coral reefs.

The Pacific islands are coping with rapid political and economic changes. The Melanesian, Micronesian and Polynesian peoples have recently founded independent states, although some islands and island groups remain overseas territories of France, the USA, Australia or New Zealand. Many of the smaller islands have had to rely on economic aid from larger countries to help them develop. Years of colonial rule brought mining and the testing of nuclear weapons to some islands, causing serious environmental damage. Today tourism and industry create some wealth, but often

N

WAKE ISLAND
(U.S.A.)

NORTHERN MARIANA
ISLANDS (U.S.A.)

GUAM
(U.S.A.)

PALAU

FEDERATED STATE
OF MICRONESIA

NAURU

IRIAN JAYA
(INDONESIA)

PAPUA NEW
GUINEA

SOLOMON
ISLANDS

TUV

Arafura Sea

Port Moresby

VANUA

Coral Sea

FI

AUSTRALIA

NEW CALEDONIA
(Fr.)

Tasman Sea

NEW
ZEALAND

Queen Alexandra's birdwing

The Queen Alexandra's birdwing is the largest butterfly in the world, with a wingspan of up to 28 cm. It is found in the tropical forests of Papua New Guinea.

WAY ISLAND
(U.S.A.)

NORTH PACIFIC
OCEAN

HAWAII
(U.S.A.)

RSHALL
LANDS

MEXICO

KIRIBATI

GALÁPAGOS
(Ecuador)

SOUTH
AMERICA

MOA

AMERICAN
SAMOA
(U.S.A)

COOK
ISLANDS
(N.Z.)

FRENCH POLYNESIA
(Fr.)

TONGA

PITCAIRN ISLAND
(U.K.)

EASTER ISLAND
(CHILE)

SOUTH PACIFIC
OCEAN

| 0 | 500 | 1000 | 1500 | 2000 Kilometres |
| 0 | 1000 | 2000 | 3000 Miles |

disrupt the traditional, self-
sufficient way of life based on
fishing and farming. However,
modern communications have
also helped to bring together
remote communities of islanders.

Unu bona boroma
● ● ● ● ● ● ● ● ● ● ● ● ● ● ● ● ● ● ● ●

*This dish from Papua New Guinea
consists of breadfruit, bacon and onions.
Breadfruit is a vegetable grown throughout
the South Pacific.*

Polynesian sculptor
● ● ● ● ● ● ● ● ● ● ● ● ● ● ● ● ● ● ● ●

A sculptor carves a stone tiki *(mythical
figure) on an island in French Polynesia.
Islanders also practise wood carving and
mat weaving.*

161

Papua New Guinea

The country of Papua New Guinea lies on the eastern half of New Guinea, the second largest island in the world. The western half of the island is part of Indonesia. Papua New Guinea also includes many small islands, such as the Bismarck Archipelago and the northern Solomon Islands. In the 1800s European traders and missionaries settled here. Germany and Britain controlled different parts of Papua New Guinea until 1920 when Australia took over. Independence finally came to the country in 1975.

Papua New Guinea is a land of mountains, fast-flowing rivers and dense forests. Its fertile soils support vast plantations of coconuts, coffee, tea, palm-oil and rubber. Grassy lowlands and marshes are home to tortoises and crocodiles. Other wildlife includes giant butterflies, large flightless birds called cassowaries and marsupials such as possums.

Most people live in rural areas, often in remote valleys that are inaccessible by road. This has meant that a huge variety of customs and languages has developed – more than 700 languages are spoken. Traditional ways of life are still strong, with communities growing their own food and hunting animals.

Kiribati

A Kiribati islander weaves a mat from strips of dried palm leaf. Coconut palms also provide fresh coconut and copra (dried coconut) for export and leaves for roofing.

American Samoa

Tuna are offloaded on the quayside at Pago Pago in American Samoa. Fishing is a major industry here, with large catches canned for export.

Fijian atoll
• • • • • • • • • • • • • • • • • • • •

This aerial view of a Fijian atoll shows clearly how an underwater mountain of coral built up over the years until its peak rose above the surface of the sea and formed an insland.

Fishing in the South Pacific
• • • • • • • • • • • • • • • • • • • •

Traditionally, islanders fish at night. They set fire to palm branches and hang them over the side of the boat. The fish swim towards the light and are speared or shot with arrows by the islanders.

Nauru

Nauru is one of the world's smallest independent countries. Most of its people live on the coast. Almost all the rest of the island consists of a plateau that once contained large deposits of phosphate rock. The phosphate was created by seabirds living on the island. Over millions of years their droppings built up to form phosphate rock. Phosphate, a valuable source of fertilizer, is Nauru's only export.

The people of Nauru used to grow their own food and farm fish in the shallow lagoons. However, 100 years of phosphate mining has reduced much of the island to desert and nearly all the island's food has to be imported. Today the government is trying to develop other industries and restore over-mined land so that it can be used for growing the island's own food again.

The Marshall Islands

These islands are named after the British sea captain John Marshall, who landed here in the late 1700s. The group consists of 31 islands and atolls. Their resources include phosphate, which is used to make fertilizers, and beautiful beaches that attract tourists. The islanders grow papaya, breadfruit and arrowroot (a starchy root).

Like other Pacific islands, the Marshall Islands have been ruled by various foreign powers. They were colonized by Germany in the 1880s, then ruled by Japan and the USA. Independence finally came in 1991.

Tuvalu

Tuvalu is made up of nine low-lying islands that form coral atolls around peaceful blue lagoons. Eight of Tuvalu's islands are inhabited. They have the highest population density in the Pacific, along with Nauru.

The islands' soil is very poor and there are few natural resources. Islanders grow bananas and taro (a starchy root) to eat and keep chickens and pigs. Fishing is also important. Coconut palms grow everywhere and copra (dried coconut kernels) is exported along with handicrafts such as woven mats and baskets. Many young islanders try to find jobs on ocean ships to earn money. Another growing source of income is charging foreign ships money to fish for tuna around the island chain. The sale of Tuvalu postage stamps to dealers also raises some income.

Micronesia

● ●

This aerial view shows some of the 600 islands that make up the Federated States of Micronesia. Rainfall here is high and the islands are subject to typhoons that often reach speeds of 240 kph.

■ NEW CALEDONIA
Area: 18,580 sq km
Population: 179,000
Capital: Nouméa (66,000)
Official language: French
Currency: Franc CFP
Main exports: Nickel, copra

■ FEDERATED STATES OF MICRONESIA
Area: 700 sq km
Population: 114,000
Capital: Palikir, on Pohnpei (7,000)
Official language: English
Currency: US dollar
Main export: Copra

■ PALAU
Area: 490 sq km
Population: 16,000
Capital: Koror (10,000)
Official languages: Palauan, English
Currency: US dollar
Main exports: Copra, tuna

■ THE MARSHALL ISLANDS
Area: 180 sq km
Population: 52,000
Capital: Majuro (20,000)
Official languages: Marshallese, English
Currency: US dollar
Main export: Copra

■ KIRIBATI
Area: 730 sq km
Population: 75,000
Capital: Bairiki, on Tarawa (25,000)
Official language: English
Currency: Australian dollar
Main exports: Copra, fish

Papua New Guinea

Palau

Solomon Islands

French Polynesia

■ NAURU
Area: 20 sq km
Population: 10,000
Seat of government: Yaren
Official language: Nauruan
Currency: Australian dollar
Main export: Phosphate

■ SOLOMON ISLANDS
Area: 28,370 sq km
Population: 354,000
Capital: Honiara (34,000)
Official language: English
Currency: Solomon Islands dollar
Main exports: Fish products, timber,
   copra, cocoa beans, palm-oil products

■ TUVALU
Area: 24 sq km
Population: 13,000
Capital: Fongafale, on Funafuti Atoll
   (3,000)
Official languages: Tuvaluan, English
Currency: Australian dollar
Main export: Copra

■ FRENCH POLYNESIA
Area: 3,270 sq km
Population: 212,000
Capital: Papeete, on Tahiti (79,000)
Official languages: French, Tahitian
Currency: Franc CFP
Main exports: Coconut oil, cultured
   pearls

■ FIJI
Area: 18,330 sq km
Population: 747,000
Capital: Suva (72,000)
Official language: English
Currency: Fiji dollar
Main exports: Sugar, gold, fish, clothes

■ SAMOA
Area: 2,830 sq km
Population: 158,000
Capital: Apia (33,000)
Official languages: Samoan, English
Currency: Tala
Main exports: Taro, coconut

■ AMERICAN SAMOA
Area: 200 sq km
Population: 38,000
Capital: Pago Pago
Official languages: Samoan, English
Currency: US dollar
Main exports: Tuna, copra

■ VANUATU
Area: 12,190 sq km
Population: 156,000
Capital: Port-Vila (20,000)
Official languages: Bislama, English,
   French
Currency: Vatu
Main exports: Copra, beef, timber

■ TONGA
Area: 750 sq km
Population: 98,000
Capital: Nukualofa (29,000)
Official languages: Tongan, English
Currency: Pa'anga
Main exports: Coconut products,
   copra, vanilla

■ PAPUA NEW GUINEA
Area: 462,840 sq km
Population: 3,922,000
Capital: Port Moresby (194,000)
Official language: English
Currency: Kina
Main exports: Gold coffee, copper,
   timber, cocoa, copra products

Federated States
of Micronesia

Marshall
Islands

Kiribati

Tuvalu

Nauru

Fiji

Samoa

American
Samoa

Vanuatu

Tonga

New Zealand

New Zealand is made up of two large islands, North Island and South Island, and a number of smaller islands, some far off in the South Pacific. This spectacular land has towering mountain ranges, lush forests, rolling grasslands and long sandy beaches. On North Island there are several active volcanoes and many hot springs and geysers. Unique species of birds, reptiles and plants have developed in New Zealand, cut off from the rest of the world by hundreds of kilometres of sea.

It is believed that the country was first settled by a people called the Maoris during the AD800s. Europeans first visited New Zealand in 1642 and started to settle in the late 1700s. Between 1840 and 1907 this country was a British colony and today most of its people are of British descent. New Zealand is now an independent country with a high

> ■ NEW ZEALAND
> *Area:* 270,530 sq km
> *Population:* 3,471,000
> *Capital:* Wellington (326,000)
> *Official language:* English
> *Currency:* New Zealand dollar
> *Main exports:* Meat, milk, butter, cheese, wool, fish, fruit

standard of living and a strong tradition of equality. In 1893 it became the first country in the world to give women the vote.

A temperate climate and plentiful rainfall make New Zealand a good farming country. Although there is some industry, the economy is largely dependent on agriculture. The meat, wool and dairy products from sheep and cattle raised on New Zealand's green pastures are exported all over the world. New Zealand's native evergreen forests are mostly protected, but extensive plantations of conifer and eucalyptus trees supply sawmills and the pulp and paper industry.

Baked kumaras

Kumaras (sweet potatoes) are a traditional Maori food. They are often baked in their jackets and served with pork and apple or with lamb.

Hydro-electric dam

This dam at Roxburgh on the Clutha River powers one of New Zealand's 30 hydro-electric schemes, which provide 75% of the country's electricity.

Whakarewarewa

Clouds of steam shoot into the air from volcanic rock at Whakarewarewa, near Rotorua on North Island. New Zealand has many geysers and hot springs. They are the result of high temperatures deep inside the Earth.

North Cape

0 50 100 150 200 250 Kilometres

0 50 100 150 Miles

N

Whangarei

Auckland

Hamilton

Waikato

Rotorua

Lake Taupo

Gisborne

New Plymouth

Mt. Ruapehu 2797m

Mt. Egmont 2518m

NORTH ISLAND

Napier

Hastings

NEW ZEALAND

Wanganui

Palmerston North

Nelson

Blenheim

■WELLINGTON

SOUTH PACIFIC OCEAN

Greymouth

Southern Alps

Tasman Sea

Aoraki (Mt. Cook)

Rakaia

Christchurch

SOUTH ISLAND

Timaru

ford und

Waitaki

Lake Te Anau

Clutha

Dunedin

Invercargill

STEWART ISLAND

Weta

The weta is a flightless insect that looks like a large grasshopper. The weta grows to about 9 cm in length and is found on Pacific islands offshore of New Zealand.

Geography

North Island has an irregular coastline fringed by inlets and sandy beaches with peninsulas projecting into the sea. Fertile lowlands rise inland to hills. The centre of North Island is a volcanic region. Four volcanoes are still active and there are many hot bubbling springs and geysers. Earthquakes are common, but rarely severe. Farther south, rugged hills descend to plains and coastal lowlands.

South Island, just 26 kilometres away across the Cook Strait, is dominated by the soaring peaks of the Southern Alps with their snowfields and glaciers. Many beautiful lakes lying in thickly forested mountain valleys feed fast-flowing rivers. To the east of the Alps lie the fertile Canterbury Plains, New Zealand's largest area of flat land. In the far southwest spectacular fiords cut narrow gashes into the land.

New Zealand is home to many unique plants, such as the scarlet-flowered pohutukawa. The native forests are mainly made up of everygreen trees and ferns. Since 1900 many new tree species have been introduced into New Zealand. The country's paper industry depends on the radiata pine, originally imported from California.

Most of New Zealand's animals have been introduced from other parts of the world. Deer, cattle and rabbits were brought by European settlers. Wallabies and brush-tailed possums came from Australia.

The kiwi, a large bird that cannot fly, is the country's national animal. Many wildlife habitats throughout the islands are now national parks.

Economy

New Zealand is a land of farms. For every person who lives here, there are about 20 farm animals. Sheep produce the country's world-famous lamb and wool. Large herds of cattle are raised for New Zealand's other major exports, beef, milk, cheese and butter. Crops include wheat, maize, barley and apples. Vineyards produce high-quality wines.

Food processing is the country's main industry. Textiles, aluminium and plastics are also manufactured. New Zealand harnesses the power of its swift-flowing rivers to produce hydro-electricity. There are also reserves of oil, natural gas, coal and gold. However, tourism has recently outstripped all the country's other ways of earning money.

The old Parliament Building with its new Executive Wing stands at the heart of Wellington, New Zealand's capital city in North Island. Wellington was founded by British settlers in 1840.

People and history

The majority of New Zealanders are descended from European settlers, mostly British, although more than 10 per cent are Maori people. The Maoris originally came from the eastern Pacific. A large part of the population is also of mixed Maori and European descent.

The first European to discover the islands was the Dutch navigator, Abel Tasman, in 1642. British settlers founded Wellington, on North Island, in 1840 and New Zealand became a British colony. After gold was discovered on South Island in 1861 a rush of settlers arrived to try and make their fortunes. During the 1860s the settlers and the Maoris quarrelled over land and a number of fierce wars occurred. As a result, the Maoris lost many of their ancestral lands and rights.

New Zealand became an independent nation in 1907, but kept its strong political and economic links with Britain. More recently the country has developed closer ties with Australia and other Pacific nations. Following a period of Maori unrest in the 1970s, there is now a new interest in Maori culture and traditions.

Tuatara
● ● ● ● ● ● ● ● ● ●

Unique to New Zealand, the tuatara is the sole survivor of a group of lizards that lived on Earth millions of years ago.

Kiwi
● ●

The kiwi leaves its burrow by night to probe for grubs and worms with its long sensitive bill, which is fringed with bristles. Although it is a bird it cannot fly. Strict laws protect the kiwi from extinction.

Australia

■ **AUSTRALIA**
Area: 7,713,364 sq km
Population: 17,662,000
Capital: Canberra (279,000)
Official language: English
Currency: Australian dollar
Main exports: Gold, other metals
and metal ores, diamonds, coal,
meat, wool, cereals

A ustralia is a vast country with a relatively small population. Most Australians live on a narrow strip of land extending along the east and southeast coasts. The interior, known as the outback, is too dry and barren to support many people. Much of it is desert or scrubby grassland where it may not rain for years at a time. However, rich deposits of minerals and grazing for vast numbers of cattle and sheep make the outback a major source of wealth for the country.

The first inhabitants of Australia were the Aboriginal peoples, who originally came from Southeast Asia about 40,000 years ago. During the 1700s Australia became a British colony and thousands of people who had committed crimes in Britain were given the choice of either going to prison or moving to Australia. As a result many Australians are of British descent and the country has maintained strong links with the UK. The head of the state is still the British monarch, but in recent years a movement to make the country a republic has gathered strength.

Funnel web spider

As its name suggests, the funnel-web spider spins a funnel-shaped web. The bite of some funnel-webs can be fatal to humans.

Broo

Ashburton

Carnarvon

**WESTE
AUSTRA**

Murchison

Geraldton

Kalgc

★**Perth**
●Fremantle

Parliament House

Australia's Parliament House in Canberra was built in 1988. Australia is a federation of six states and two territories. It has a federal government that decides national issues, and separate state governments.

Three Sisters Rock

The Three Sisters are an unusual rock formation at Katoomba near Sydney in New South Wales. The rock has been eroded to leave three pinnacles.

Lamingtons

Lamingtons are a teatime treat in Australia. They are squares of sponge cake covered in chocolate and coconut. Most Australian recipes originate in Europe.

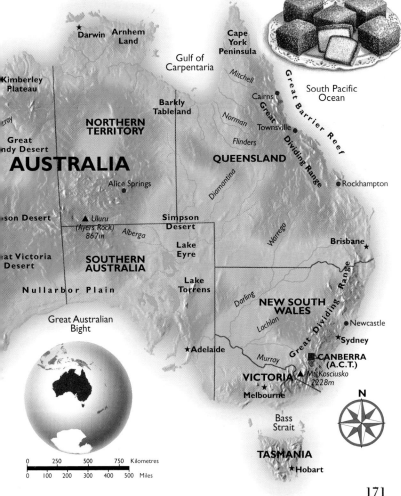

Darwin

Arnhem Land

Cape York Peninsula

Gulf of Carpentaria

Mitchell

South Pacific Ocean

Kimberley Plateau

zroy

Cairns

Great Barrier Reef

Barkly Tableland

NORTHERN TERRITORY

Norman

Townsville

Great Dividing Range

Great ndy Desert

Flinders

QUEENSLAND

AUSTRALIA

Alice Springs

Rockhampton

son Desert

▲ Uluru (Ayers Rock) 867m

Alberga

Diamantina

Simpson Desert

at Victoria Desert

SOUTHERN AUSTRALIA

Lake Eyre

Warrego

Brisbane ★

Lake Torrens

Great Dividing Range

Nullarbor Plain

Darling

NEW SOUTH WALES

Great Australian Bight

Lachlan

●Newcastle

★Adelaide

Murray

★Sydney

■CANBERRA (A.C.T.)

VICTORIA
★

▲ Mt Kosciusko 2228m

Melbourne
★

Bass Strait

N

| 0 | 250 | 500 | 750 | Kilometres |

| 0 | 100 | 200 | 300 | 400 | 500 | Miles |

TASMANIA

★Hobart

Geography

The wettest, most fertile areas of Australia are concentrated along the coastline. The northern coast is tropical and humid, with lush rainforests and mangrove swamps. The fertile strip along the east and southeast coasts rises to the rocky Great Dividing Range. The highest peaks of this range are known as the Australian Alps.

West of the Great Dividing Range lie vast plains broken by occasional rocky hills. The landscape includes scrub, sparse pasture and dried-out river beds. Water from wells enables livestock to be grazed there. Beyond these plains a huge plateau covers the western two thirds of Australia. Much of this interior is a baking wilderness of stone and cracked clay. However, the southwest coast enjoys warm dry summers and moist winters. The mountainous island of Tasmania lies southeast of the mainland.

Economy

Most of Australia's wealth has come from farming and mining. Although much of the country is too dry for growing crops, the vast grasslands are ideal for grazing large numbers of sheep and cattle. Crops such as wheat, sugarcane and fruit are grown on only about five per cent of the farmland, but this land is highly productive because of modern farming methods. Australia's major farming exports include wool, meat and dairy products, as well as wines made from grapes grown in the south.

Since the 1800s Australia has exported large amounts of minerals, including gold, copper, silver and zinc. Huge deposits of bauxite (used to make aluminium), iron ore and coal were discovered in the 1950s and oil and gas were found in the 1960s. Today a larger part of the Australian workforce is employed in service industries.

Boomerang and shield

Aboriginals have used boomerangs for hunting for thousands of years. If thrown properly, a boomerang will come back. The boomerang and shield are made of decorated wood.

Surfing

Surfing is one of Australia's most popular sports. For outdoor pursuits, Australians wear sunscreen cream to protect their skin against burning in the fierce sun.

People

The Aboriginals were the first to live in Australia. The word aboriginal means 'there in the beginning'. The Aboriginals lived a nomadic life, hunting and gathering food wherever they went. Today only one and a half per cent of Australians belong to this ethnic group and very few follow the traditional way of life. In recent years some Aboriginals have campaigned successfully for rights to the land that was taken from them by European settlers.

Opals

Opals are iridescent stones used in jewellery. The finest opals in the world are mined in northern New South Wales, Australia.

Kangaroo

The kangaroo is a marsupial, a mammal that carries its baby in its pouch. Kangaroos live on grassy plains and move about in troops, springing on their powerful hind legs.

Sydney Opera House

Sydney Opera House was designed by Danish architect Jørn Utzon and completed in 1973. It is set on a spectacular site in Sydney Harbour.

Most Australians originally came from Europe. By far the greatest proportion came from Britain and Ireland, but large numbers of Greeks, Italians and Slavs also settled here. Since the 1950s the Australian way of life has been enriched by the traditions, customs and foods of other immigrant groups, including the peoples of southeast Asia and Japan.

ANTARCTICA

Antarctica is the world's fifth continent and its coldest by far. Its landscape and climate are so harsh that people have never settled here permanently. Its only inhabitants are visiting scientists who carry out research projects. The first people to cross the Antarctic Circle were probably Maoris from New Zealand. In 1773 the English navigator James Cook also crossed the Antarctic Circle, but he never sighted land. The mainland was first sighted in the early 1800s and the South Pole was finally reached by a Norwegian, Roald Amundsen, in 1911.

Antarctica is not owned by any country. However, it is rich in minerals and fish, so various nations have made claims here. Thirty-eight countries support a treaty signed in 1959 encouraging scientific research and peace in Antarctica. In 1991 mining was banned for 50 years in an effort to keep this wilderness unspoilt and unexploited by people. In recent years scientists working in Antarctica to monitor climatic changes have reported a thinning of the ozone layer here. Ozone is a gas, high in the Earth's atmosphere, that protects life on Earth from harmful ultra-violet rays, which can scorch crops and cause skin cancer. The ozone layer is being destroyed by the use of chemicals such as CFCs.

■ CONTINENTAL FACTS

Area: 14,000,000 sq km
Population: No permanent population
Highest point: Vinson Massif (4,897 m)
Ice cover: Ice and snow cover 98% of Antarctica
Average depth of ice: 2,000 m
Deepest ice: 4,800 m
Mineral resources: In 1991 commercial mining was banned for 50 years
Living resources: Cod, icefish, krill

Emperor penguin

The emperor is one of two species of penguins that nest on the ice shelves of Antarctica. Six other species visit Antarctic waters, but they choose to nest and breed on remote islands.

Icebreaker

Only icebreakers can safely navigate around icebergs. Nine-tenths of their bulk is submerged beneath the Antarctic waters.

0 500 1000 1500 2000 Kilometres
0 250 500 750 1000 1250 Miles

SOUTH ATLANTIC OCEAN

Antarctic Peninsula

Queen Maud Land

Weddell Sea

Enderby Land

INDIAN OCEAN

Ronne Ice Shelf

Trans-Antarctic Mountains

▲ *Vinson Massif* 5140m

● **South Pole**

Ellsworth Land

Ross Ice Shelf

▲ *Mt. Erebus* 3794m

Wilkes Land

Victoria Land

Ross Sea

SOUTH PACIFIC OCEAN

Antarctic Circle

Roald Amundsen

* *

The Norwegian explorer, Roald Amundsen, plants his country's flag at the South Pole. Amundsen's expedition was the first to reach the Pole. It arrived on 14 December 1911.

175

THE ARCTIC

The Arctic Circle is an imaginary line around the northern part of the globe. Within this desolate area lies the Arctic Ocean, which is frozen over for much of the year. When the ice breaks up in spring it forms huge floes (fields of ice). Parts of the ocean never melt, but create a great ice cap round the North Pole.

The Arctic Ocean is bordered by Greenland and the northern parts of Canada, Alaska, Russia and Scandinavia. The people of these snowy lands include the Inuit (Eskimos) of Greenland, North America and northeast Asia, the Aleuts of Alaska, the Lapps of Scandinavia and the Yakuts and Chukchee of Russia. Some of them still follow a traditional way of life, hunting fish, seals and whales, or herding reindeer, which they keep for meat, milk and hides.

There are many islands in the Arctic, some of them mountainous, and treeless plains called tundra cover a wide area. During the brief summer on the tundra flowers bloom and scrubby plants provide grazing for caribou and reindeer. The Arctic Ocean is rich in plankton, which are devoured by whales. Fish are preyed on by walruses and seals, which in turn are hunted by polar bears.

Russians and Scandinavians were exploring the Arctic from the 1600s onwards, some searching for a sea route around North America to China. The first person to reach the North Pole was Robert Peary of the US Navy in 1909.

■ THE ARCTIC
Area (Arctic Ocean):
 9,500,000 sq km
Average depth of Ocean: 1,300 m
Deepest point: 5,450 m
Mineral resources: Oil, natural
 gas, coal
Living resources: Fish, seals

■ GREENLAND
Area: 2,175,600 sq km
Population: 55,000
Capital: Godthaab (11,000)
Official languages: Danish,
 Greenlandic
Currency: Danish krone
Main exports: Fish, cryolite, skins

Arctic tern

The Arctic tern breeds on Arctic coasts, then migrates further than any other bird, to the Antarctic at the other end of the world.

Polar bear

Polar bears live on Arctic coasts. They are strong swimmers. Their fur and fat protect them against the icy waters.

176

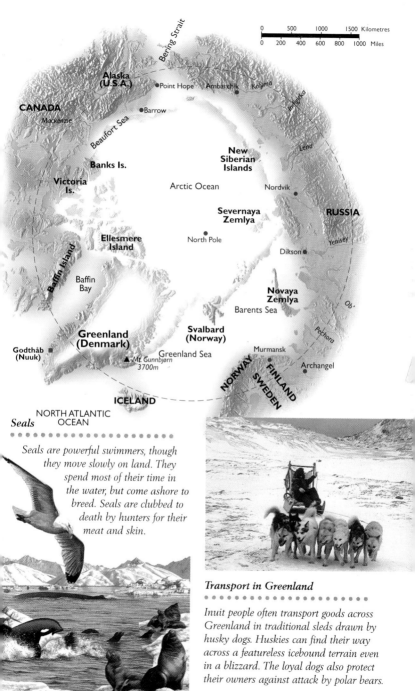

Map labels

Bering Strait

0 500 1000 1500 Kilometres
0 200 400 600 800 1000 Miles

Alaska
(U.S.A.)
Point Hope • Ambarchik • Kolyma

Indigirka

CANADA
Mackenzie
• Barrow

Beaufort Sea

New
Siberian
Islands

Lena

Banks Is.

Arctic Ocean

Nordvik

Victoria
Is.

Severnaya
Zemlya

RUSSIA

Ellesmere
Island

North Pole

Yenisey

Baffin Island

Dikson •

Baffin
Bay

Novaya
Zemlya

Barents Sea

Ob'

Greenland
(Denmark)

Svalbard
(Norway)

Pechora

Godthåb ■
(Nuuk)

Greenland Sea
▲ Mt Gunnbjørn
3700m

Murmansk

Archangel

NORWAY

FINLAND

SWEDEN

ICELAND

NORTH ATLANTIC
OCEAN

Seals

Seals are powerful swimmers, though
they move slowly on land. They
spend most of their time in
the water, but come ashore to
breed. Seals are clubbed to
death by hunters for their
meat and skin.

Transport in Greenland

Inuit people often transport goods across
Greenland in traditional sleds drawn by
husky dogs. Huskies can find their way
across a featureless icebound terrain even
in a blizzard. The loyal dogs also protect
their owners against attack by polar bears.

177

GLOSSARY

W ords in italics have
their own separate
glossary entry.

*Currency is the type of
money a country uses, such
as rupees in India and
dollars in the USA.*

■ **Acid rain** Rain that has been
made very acidic by waste gases
from factories and cars. These
gases pollute the atmosphere and
also pollute rainfall. Acid rain can
cause great damage to plants and
animals. It can even damage the
surface of buildings.

■ **Agriculture** Using land for
growing crops and/or for keeping
and grazing animals.

■ **Ancestor** Relative from whom
a person is descended, such as a
great-great grandparent.

■ **Apartheid** Policy of separating
and keeping apart people from
different races.

■ **Archipelago** Group of islands.

■ **Atoll** Coral reef or islands that
form a partial or complete ring
around a *lagoon*.

■ **Atomic bomb** Highly
destructive bomb. Its energy
comes from splitting tiny
chemical particles called atoms.

■ **Bauxite** A raw material used to
make aluminium.

■ **Cash crop** Crop grown to sell
rather than to feed the grower's
own family.

■ **Cassava** Tropical plant with
starchy roots. The root is dried
and pounded to make flour for
bread and tapioca for puddings.

■ **Censorship** System that
prevents the communication of
certain ideas in words or pictures.

■ **Civil war** War between
opposing groups of people within
the same country.

■ **Colony** Area taken over or
settled by people who have
invaded from another country.

■ **Communism** Political system
where land, industry and all
property and goods are controlled
by the government or *state*.

■ **Copra** Dried coconut kernels
from which an oil is extracted.

■ **Currency** Type of money used
within a country, such as rupees
in India and dollars in USA.

■ **Cyclone** Very stormy weather
with violent spiralling winds. A
tropical cyclone is another name
for a *hurricane*.

■ **Deforestation** Loss of areas of
forest. Some forests are cut down
for their timber. Others may be
cleared to make way for buildings
or agriculture. In many parts of
the world, conservationists are
carrying out projects to replace
trees and protect forests.

■ **Delta** Area at the mouth of a
river where the stream of water
divides into several channels,
flowing through deposits of sand
and mud.

■ **Democracy** System of
government where the people
have a certain amount of power
because they elect those who
govern them.

■ **Democratic election** Election that allows the people of a country to choose who governs them. Each person has one vote.

■ **Dependency** Area of land that is controlled or supported by another country.

■ **Descendant** Person who comes from particular *ancestors*. You are a descendant of your great-great-great grandparents.

■ **Dike (or dyke)** Bank or wall built to hold back the sea or a river to prevent flooding. The word is also used for a channel or a ditch dug to drain wet land.

■ **Drought** A long period of dry weather that causes a severe shortage of water.

■ **Economy** The way a country produces, uses and distributes its goods and services.

■ **Elder** Older person in a community who is greatly respected for knowledge and wisdom gained over a lifetime.

■ **Empire** Group of *colonies* or *territories* that is controlled by a country or power.

Deltas at the mouths of rivers are often shaped like the Greek letter Δ ('D', called delta in Greek). This is how they got their name.

■ **Equator** Imaginary line around the middle of the Earth, at an equal distance from the North and South Poles.

■ **Erosion** Wearing away of rock, land or buildings by running water, ice, winds or sea waves.

■ **Ethnic group** Group of people with distinguishing characteristics, such as language, religion, racial origin or customs.

■ **Exploit** a) To develop land or resources; b) to use land, resources or people for selfish reasons. Colonists in many parts of the world have often got rich by exploiting people and local natural resources.

■ **Export** Product made in one country and sold to another.

■ **Extinct** No longer in existence. Groups of people, animals and plants that have died out and volcanoes that no longer erupt are said to be extinct.

■ **Famine** An extreme shortage of food that may lead to people dying of starvation.

■ **Federal** A system where a nation is divided into several *states*, *provinces* or *territories*. Each separate area is self-governing in local matters, while a central government decides national matters.

■ **Fiord** Narrow, deep and steep-sided inlet of the sea in a mountainous area.

■ **Fossil** Remains or evidence of an animal or plant that lived a long time ago. Fossils are usually found hardened in rock.

■ **Free market** Economic system where the government does not control the *economy*.

179

■ **Geyser** Natural hot spring that throws up jets of steam or hot water out of the ground.

■ **Glacier** Huge mass of ice that moves slowly downhill, along a river valley. Glaciers form high up in the mountains, where the snow piles up year after year.

■ **Gorge** Deep, narrow, steep-sided valley.

■ **Guerrilla** Member of a group of armed rebels fighting against the controlling force of a country.

■ **Habitat** The specific natural surroundings in which animals and plants live.

■ **Humid** Moist or damp, as in air or climate.

■ **Hurricane** Storm with winds that travel at speeds of more than 120 km per hour.

■ **Hydro-electric power** Electricity made by using the power of water from rivers or lakes that have been dammed.

■ **Ice Age** Period of time on a planet when temperatures are extremely low for a very long time. Ice Ages took place on Earth long ago and lasted millions of years. The last one ended around 10,000 years ago.

■ **Import** Product that is brought into a country from abroad.

■ **Inflation** Overall rise in the price of goods and services. This in turn leads to a fall in the value of money. When money is devalued, it means that more is needed to buy the same goods.

■ **Intensive farming** Ways of getting the greatest amount of agricultural produce possible from a piece of land. Intensive farming methods include using

A gorge is a deep, narrow, steep-sided valley. This is Samaria Gorge in Crete.

chemical fertilizers and pesticides and modern farming machinery, as well as rearing large numbers of animals in a small space.

■ **Investment** Money that people put into developing a project such as a business or industry.

■ **Irrigation** System for providing a supply of water to crops where rainfall is poor.

■ **Lagoon** Freshwater or saltwater lake that is separated from the sea by a sandbank or coral reef.

■ **Land reclamation** Bringing flooded or wasteland back into use by either draining or clearing.

■ **Legislation** The laws of a country and how these laws are drawn up and put into practice.

■ **Manufacturing industry** Large-scale factory production of a wide range of goods.

■ **Military rule** Government by the armed forces of a country.

■ **Mineral** Naturally occurring substance found in the ground. Gold, coal, precious stones and salt are all minerals. They are valuable *natural resources*.

■ **Monarchy** Land ruled by a king, queen, emperor or empress. Monarchs have varying degrees of power. In a constitutional monarchy most of the power is held by a *democratically elected* government. A monarch's title is hereditary, which means that it is passed down from one generation to the next.

■ **Monsoon** Extremely strong seasonal wind that can be accompanied by very wet stormy weather. The best-known monsoons occur in southern Asia. They blow from the land to the sea in winter and from the sea to the land in summer.

■ **Multiparty election** Election in which voters can choose between several different political groups or parties.

■ **Native** Person born and living in a particular area.

■ **Natural resource** Part of the natural environment, such as fertile land and minerals, that can be used to produce something else. A workforce of people is also a natural resource.

A nomad is someone who regularly moves from place to place in search of food or grazing for animals such as camels or goats. Nomads sleep in tents made of the skin or felted hair of their animals. They live off the meat and milk of their herds and sell the hides.

■ **Navigation** The skill of trying to find the easiest, quickest route from one place to another. The term is used in reference to sea, air and land travel.

■ **Nomad** Person who regularly moves from place to place in search of food or grazing for animals such as camels, reindeer, sheep or goats. The land where nomads live is usually not hospitable or fertile enough to support settled communities.

■ **Nuclear power** Energy released by causing reactions to take place within the nuclei (central parts) of atoms. This energy can be produced and used in power stations to provide electricity.

■ **Peninsula** Area of land jutting out from the mainland and surrounded by sea on three sides.

■ **Pesticide** Poison that is used to kill pests and weeds that interfere with crop-growing. Many people are looking for alternatives to pesticides, because they can cause a lot of damage to the environment, and sometimes to humans and other animals.

■ **Petrochemical industry** Manufacturing industry using chemicals that are made from crude oil or natural gas. Products of this industry include plastics, fertilizers and medicines.

■ **Plain** Large area of flat land.

■ **Plantation** Large farm or estate where valuable *cash crops* such as tea, coffee, sugar or cotton are grown. Just one crop is often grown on a plantation.

■ **Plateau** Large area of flat or fairly flat land that is raised above the surrounding country.

■ **Poaching** Stealing animals from private land. These animals may be prized as food, or for some other valuable product. Many poachers steal animals that are endangered or protected by the law. For example, elephants are killed for their ivory tusks and certain birds and monkeys are stolen so they can be sold as pets.

■ **Pollution** The result of damaging the air, land or water with harmful substances. These substances include waste products from industry, power stations, cars and *intensive farming* methods.

■ **Principality** Area of land ruled by a prince. As with a *monarchy*, the ruler may have a small or large amount of real power.

■ **Protectorate** Area of land that is under the protection and partial control of another country.

■ **Province** Area of land that is part of a country or *empire*.

■ **Public spending** The spending of money collected from the people in taxes. The government decides how this will be spent.

■ **Racism** Unfair treatment of one race by another because of unreasonable fear or hatred. As a result people may be insulted or attacked, denied jobs, decent housing and education.

■ **Raw material** Natural substance that can be made into other products. Iron ore is a raw material used to make steel.

■ **Refinery** Factory where *raw materials* are broken down and processed so that they can be used to make other products. Crude oil is refined to make petroleum and other fuels.

■ **Refugee** Person forced to flee his or her home country. This might be because of war, famine or religious or political beliefs.

■ **Republic** Country where the people vote for the head of state, who is often the head of the government. The country is usually headed by a president, rather than a monarch. In a democratic republic the people elect their government from a choice of political parties.

■ **Revolution** Overthrow of an existing system of government replacing it with another. Force and violence are frequently used to achieve this.

■ **Riot** Disturbance that involves a crowd of people. A riot may be very violent.

■ **Sanction** Action taken by a government as a way of making a protest against an organization or country. A sanction usually restricts trade and therefore limits income. Several countries might refuse to trade with another country where a certain group of people are being treated very badly. Sanctions are taken in the hope that they will force the country to change its policies.

■ **Savanna** Large grassy region, found in tropical or sub-tropical areas, where few or no trees grow.

■ **Service industry** Industry providing services for people rather than goods. Tourism, healthcare, entertainment, education, catering and banking are all service industries.

■ **Settler** Someone who goes to live permanently in an undeveloped area.

■ **Shaman** Priest or priest-doctor figure found mainly in Asia.

■ **Shanty town** Area of poor, makeshift dwellings, usually on the edge of a town. These areas grow up because there is not enough housing for everyone in the town.

■ **Shrine** Holy place with a special meaning for a certain religious group.

■ **Slash-and-burn agriculture** Growing crops on land that has been cleared by cutting down trees and burning plant life. Land that has been cleared like this does not stay fertile for very long and so the people move on to slash and burn a new plot.

■ **Slavery** Buying and selling of humans, who then become the property of the buyer. Slaves are denied freedom and forced to work without payment.

■ **Sorghum** A kind of grass that produces a nourishing grain used to make bread.

■ **State** Large community that is organized under one local or national government. The word is also used to mean the government of a country, especially a communist country.

■ **Strike** A period when workers stop working to protest against low wages or poor conditions.

■ **Subsidy** Money given by governments to certain industries or organizations to keep prices down or improve production.

■ **Subsistence farming** A method by which farmers can grow only enough food to support themselves and their families, with few or no extra crops to sell.

■ **Territory** When it is used as an official term, territory means an area of land that is controlled by a *state* or country.

■ **Terrorist** Someone who tries to achieve political ends by using violence and intimidation.

■ **Trawling** Method of catching large numbers of fish by dragging a big, wide-mouthed net through the sea.

■ **Tributary** River that flows into another, larger river.

■ **Tsunami** Wave caused by an earthquake on the seabed.

■ **Tundra** Treeless *plain* in the far north that supports mainly mosses, lichens and small hardy shrubs. The subsoil of the tundra (soil beneath the top layer) is permanently frozen.

■ **Typhoon** Another name for a small violent storm or *cyclone*.

■ **Veld** Large stretch of open grassland found in parts of southern Africa.

Trawling is a common method of catching fish. A net is dragged behind a fishing vessel called a trawler.

183

INDEX

187

188

ACKNOWLEDGEMENTS

The publishers would like to thank the following sources for providing photographs: PAGE 10/11 (TR) © 1996 Corel Corp.; 15 (BR) David Woodfall/Tony Stone Images; 18 (C) Christopher Morris/ Black Star!Colorific!; 19 (BR) Alexandra Avakin/Woodfin Camp World/Telegraph Colour Library; 20 (TR) John Lawrence/ Tony Stone Images; 21 (BR) Hugh Sitton/Tony Stone Images; 21 (BR) Alan Kearney/Tony Stone Images; 26 (BR) Steffan Widstrand/Bruce Coleman Ltd.; 27 (TR) Canadian Tourist Office; 28 (BL) ZEFA; 31 (CR) ZEFA; 32/3 (C) Robert Frerck/Tony Stone Worldwide; 38 (TR) David Hiser/Tony Stone Worldwide; 39 (CR) John Adriaan/ Tony Stone Worldwide; 39 (B) Sarah Stone/Tony Stone; 41 (TL) Spectrum Colour Library; 44 (CL) Ingrid Morato/Panos Pictures; 44 (BR) © Tayacan/Panos Pictures; 47 (TR) Guyana Space Centre/South American Pictures; 49 (TL) ZEFA; 53 (TR) M.Barlow/Trip; 53 (L) Julio Etchart/Panos Pictures; 54 (TR) Corbis; 58 (BR) Finnish Tourist Board; 59 (TL) © Goran Assner/Swedish Travel & Tourism Council; 63 (TL) Walter Rawlings/ Robert Harding Picture Library; 63 (TR) ZEFA; 67 (CR) Dennis Gilbert/Larousse; 67 (CL) ZEFA; 70 (TR) Ed Pritchard/Tony Stone Worldwide; 71 (B) Robert Harding Picture Library; 72 (TR) Andy Price/Bruce Coleman Ltd.; 73 (BR) Robert Harding Picture Library; 74 (B) Fred Frieberg/Robert Harding Picture Library; 75 (TR) Adam Woolfitt/Robert Harding Picture Library; 75 (TR) Bill O'Connor/ Robert Harding Picture Library; 76 (TR) Walter Rawlings/Robert Harding Picture Library; 78 (CL) ZEFA; 79 (T) ZEFA; 81 (BR) Robert Harding Picture Library; 83 (TR) Sean Egan/Tony Stone Images; 83 (TC) Robert Everts/ Tony Stone Worldwide; 85 (TR) J. Allan Cash; 85 (B) Jean-Leo Dugast/Panos Pictures; 87 (B) World Pictures/Feature Pix; 88 (BR) Corbis; 90 (BL) Corbis; 90/1 (CT) Joe Cornish/Tony Stone Worldwide; 92 (B) George Grigoriou/Tony Stone Images; 96 (BL) Liam Muir; 98 (BL) Corbis; 99(TL) Corbis; 100 (TL) A.Boulat/ Sipa Press/Rex Features; 101 (BR) V.Shuba/Trip; 104 (TC) Ben Aris/ Panos Pictures; 106 (TL) Lehtikuvoy/Rex Features; 113 (TL) Spectrum Colour Library; 113 (C) Julian Calder/Tony Stone Worldwide; 114/5 (T) ZEFA; 115 (BR) ZEFA; 117 (TR) © 1996 Corel Corp; 118 (B) Paul Chesley/ Tony Stone Images; 121 (TR) Robert McLeod/Robert Harding Picture Library; 122-134 all photographs from Corbis; 137 (BR) Andrew Hill/The Hutchison Library; 143 (TL) Christine Osborne Pictures; 143 (BR) Thierry Borredon/Tony Stone Images; 149 (C) Horniman Museum/Bridgeman Art Library; 153 (BL) Howard Davies/Panos Pictures; 162/3 (C) Tony Stone Worldwide; 164 (BL) Paul Chesley/Tony Stone Worldwide; 168/9 (TC) Robert Harding Picture Library; 171 (TL) Corbis; 173 (TR) Corbis; 174 © Fotex/Drewer/Rex Features; 177 both photographs Rex Features.